First World War
and Army of Occupation
War Diary
France, Belgium and Germany

40 DIVISION
119 Infantry Brigade
Royal Inniskilling Fusiliers
13th Battalion
10 June 1918 - 30 April 1919

WO95/2606/1

The Naval & Military Press Ltd
www.nmarchive.com
Published in association with The National Archives

Published by

The Naval & Military Press Ltd

Unit 10 Ridgewood Industrial Park,

Uckfield, East Sussex,

TN22 5QE England

Tel: +44 (0) 1825 749494

www.naval-military-press.com

www.nmarchive.com

This diary has been reprinted in facsimile from the original. Any imperfections are inevitably reproduced and the quality may fall short of modern type and cartographic standards.

© **Crown Copyright**
Images reproduced by permission of The National Archives, London, England, 2015.

Contents

Document type	Place/Title	Date From	Date To
Heading	WO95/2606/1 13 Battalion Royal Inniskilling Fusiliers		
Heading	40th Division 119th Infy Bde 13th Bn Roy, Innis Fus. Jun 1918-Apr 1919 In France Formed June 1918		
Heading	War Diary Of 13th Bn. Royal Inniskilling Fusiliers From 10/6/18 To 30/6/18 (Volume 1)		
War Diary	Etaples	10/06/1918	10/06/1918
War Diary	Watten	10/06/1918	10/06/1918
War Diary	Wulverdinghe	10/06/1918	15/06/1918
War Diary	Nieurlet	15/06/1918	23/06/1918
War Diary	St. Omer Sheet 27 U.17.c.7.8.	23/06/1918	30/06/1918
Miscellaneous	Defence Scheme.	29/06/1918	29/06/1918
War Diary	Sheet 27 U 17 C. 7.8.	01/07/1918	03/07/1918
War Diary	V. 15.a.9.1.	03/07/1918	07/07/1918
War Diary	U17.C.9.8.	08/07/1918	14/07/1918
War Diary	Sheet 27 U.17.c.9.8.	15/07/1918	17/07/1918
War Diary	W.25	18/07/1918	18/07/1918
War Diary	Tiflis House E 5a.0.9	19/07/1918	23/07/1918
War Diary	V24.d.4.8.	23/07/1918	27/07/1918
War Diary	E.3.c.1.7.	27/07/1918	30/07/1918
War Diary	U.17.	31/07/1918	31/07/1918
Heading	War Diary Of. 13th Bn. Royal Inniskilling Fusiliers From 1/8/1918 To 31/8/1918 (Volume 1)		
War Diary	Sheet 27 U.17.c.7.8.	01/08/1918	21/08/1918
War Diary	Le Tir Anglais	22/08/1918	22/08/1918
War Diary	Sheet 36a NE E 23 B	23/08/1918	30/08/1918
War Diary	D.21.a.	31/08/1918	31/08/1918
Miscellaneous	13th Bn Royal Inniskilling Fusiliers.	26/08/1918	26/08/1918
Miscellaneous	13th Bn. Roy. Inniskilling Fus.	28/08/1918	28/08/1918
Heading	War Diary Of 13th Bn. Royal Inniskilling Fusiliers From 1/9/1918 To 30/9/1918 (Volume 1)		
War Diary	Sheet 36a D. 21.a.	01/09/1918	02/09/1918
War Diary	Vieux Berquin	03/09/1918	04/09/1918
War Diary	Le Chien Blanc	04/09/1918	06/09/1918
War Diary	Lett Farm. B. 25.C.3.6.	07/09/1918	08/09/1918
War Diary	Lett Farm	08/09/1918	10/09/1918
War Diary	Poston Farm B. 19.b.3.4.	11/09/1918	14/09/1918
War Diary	Le Chien Blanc A.21.d.4.5.	14/09/1918	21/09/1918
War Diary	Hazebrouck	21/09/1918	26/09/1918
War Diary	Sheet 36. N.W. B. 10.Z.25.20.	27/09/1918	30/09/1918
War Diary	B.12.b.4.4.	30/09/1918	30/09/1918
Operation(al) Order(s)	B Bn Roy Innis Operation Order No. 16		
Operation(al) Order(s)	Bn. Royal Inniskilling Fusiliers. Operation Order No. 17.	02/09/1918	02/09/1918
Operation(al) Order(s)	13th Bn Royal Inniskilling Fus. Operation Order No. 18	05/09/1918	05/09/1918
Operation(al) Order(s)	13th Bn Royal Innis Fus. Operation Order 19.	13/09/1918	13/09/1918
Operation(al) Order(s)	13th Bn Royal Inniskilling Fuslrs Operation Order No. 20	18/09/1918	18/09/1918
Operation(al) Order(s)	13th Bn. Royal Inniskilling Fusiliers Operation No. 21	20/09/1918	20/09/1918
Operation(al) Order(s)	13th Bn. Royal Inniskilling Fusiliers Operation No. 21		
Operation(al) Order(s)	13th Bn. Royal Inniskilling Fusiliers Operation No. 23.		

Type	Description	Date From	Date To
Miscellaneous	For Operations On 27th August 1918 At Vieux Berquin.	12/09/1918	12/09/1918
Miscellaneous	13th Bn Inniskilling Fusiliers Operation Order No.	30/09/1918	30/09/1918
Heading	War Diary 13th R. Inniskilling Fus Month Of October Vol 5		
Heading	War Diary Of The 13th Bn. Royal Inniskilling Fusiliers From 1/10/18 To 31/10/18 (Volume 1)		
War Diary	Sheet 36 N.W. B 12.b.4.5.	01/10/1918	01/10/1918
War Diary	C. 13.b.6.2.	02/10/1918	02/10/1918
War Diary	Lys Post	03/10/1918	03/10/1918
War Diary	Le Bizet	03/10/1918	05/10/1918
War Diary	B.10.b.0.5.	06/10/1918	07/10/1918
War Diary	B.9.a.8.6.	08/10/1918	11/10/1918
War Diary	Le Chien Blanc	13/10/1918	16/10/1918
War Diary	B.9.d.8.6.	17/10/1918	17/10/1918
War Diary	36NE/J.I.a.9.1.	18/10/1918	24/10/1918
War Diary	Bondues	24/10/1918	31/10/1918
Miscellaneous		04/10/1918	04/10/1918
Miscellaneous	Headquarters 119th Infantry Brigade.		
Miscellaneous	13th Bn Royal Inniskilling Fusiliers. Sheet For Defence Of Nieppe System.	10/10/1918	10/10/1918
Miscellaneous	13th Bn Royal Inniskilling Fusiliers. Operation Order No. 25	10/10/1918	10/10/1918
Miscellaneous	119th Inf. Bde.	11/10/1918	11/10/1918
Operation(al) Order(s)	13th R. Innis Fus. Operation Order No. 24	11/10/1918	11/10/1918
Miscellaneous	C Form. Messages And Signals.		
Operation(al) Order(s)	13th Bn. Royal Inniskilling Fuslrs. Operation Order No. 26	17/10/1918	17/10/1918
Miscellaneous	C Form. Messages And Signals.		
Operation(al) Order(s)	13th Bn. Royal Inniskilling Fusiliers Operation Order No. 27	23/10/1918	23/10/1918
Miscellaneous	Addendum To Operation Order No. 27	23/10/1918	23/10/1918
Miscellaneous	C Form. Messages And Signals.		
Miscellaneous			
Operation(al) Order(s)	13th Bn Royal Innis. Fuslrs Operation Order No. 28	25/10/1918	25/10/1918
Operation(al) Order(s)	13th Bn. R. Innis Fus. Operation Order No. 29	31/10/1918	31/10/1918
Miscellaneous	C Form. Messages And Signals.		
Heading	War Diary Of 13th Bn Royal Inniskilling Fusiliers From 1/11/18 To 30/11/18. (Volume I)		
War Diary	Wattrelos	01/11/1918	01/11/1918
War Diary	Nechin	02/11/1918	09/11/1918
War Diary	Sheet 37. I.4.a	09/11/1918	10/11/1918
War Diary	Bois De Chin	11/11/1918	15/11/1918
War Diary	Croix	16/11/1918	30/11/1918
Heading	War Diary Of The B. Bn. Royal Inniskilling Fusiliers From 1/12/18 To 31/12/18 (Volume I)		
War Diary	Croix	01/12/1918	31/12/1918
War Diary	Croix Trance	01/01/1919	31/01/1919
Heading	War Diary Of The 13th Bn. Royal Innis. Fus. 1st To 28th Feb. 1919 (Volume II)		
War Diary	Croix	01/02/1919	28/02/1919
Heading	13th Bn. R. Innis Fus. War Diary March. 1919 Vol II		
War Diary	Croix	01/03/1919	30/03/1919
Heading	War Diary Of The 13th Battn. The Royal Inniskilling Fusiliers. From 1st April 1919. To 30th April 1919. Volume II.		

War Diary   Croix France (Nord)   01/04/1919   30/04/1919

WO 95/2606/1
13 Battalion Royal Inniskilling Fusiliers

40TH DIVISION
119TH INFY BDE

13TH BN ROY. INNIS FUS.

JUN 1918- APR 1919

FORMED in France JUNE 1918

119/40

Confidential

War diary
of

13th Bn. Royal Inniskilling Fusiliers

From 10/6/18 to 30/6/18

(Volume 1)

Army Form C. 2118.

WAR DIARY
or
INTELLIGENCE SUMMARY.
(Erase heading not required.)

Instructions regarding War Diaries and Intelligence Summaries are contained in F. S. Regs., Part II. and the Staff Manual respectively. Title pages will be prepared in manuscript.

Place	Date	Hour	Summary of Events and Information	Remarks and references to Appendices
ETAPLES	10/6/18	1.20 am	Headquarters establishment entrained	
WATTEN	10/6/18		Detrained and marched to WULVERDINGHE	
WULVERDINGHE	10/6/18		Arrived billets	
"	11/6/18		Carried on with organisation	
"	12/6/18		do	
"	13/6/18		do	
"	14/6/18		do	
"	15/6/18	10.45 am	Left WULVERDINGHE by march route	
NIEURLET	15/6/18	3 p.m.	Arrived	
"	16/6/18		4 Companies - (G.H.I.J) arrived Strength 17 officers 784 O.R. - billets close to officers:- A/Capt. ROXBURGH W.R.P. A/Capt. HICKS C.H. Lieut. McLEOD N. 2/Lieut. MOSS W.F. 2/Lieut. PARRY J.G.M. 2/Lieut. CAREW C.V.E. 2/Lieut. KILROE F.J. 2/Lieut. PARR S.H. 2/Lieut. FISHLEY P.T. 2/Lieut. SMILES S. 2/Lieut. SUMMERHAYES J.A.S. 2/Lieut. WATSON R. 2/Lieut. EAGLE-BOTT C.H. 2/Lieut. BAKER A.H. 2/Lieut. CHAMPNEY F.A. 2/Lieut. HUDSON F.A.A. 2/Lieut. WYLIE W.H.	

Army Form C. 2118.

WAR DIARY
or
INTELLIGENCE SUMMARY.
(Erase heading not required.)

Place	Date	Hour	Summary of Events and Information	Remarks and references to Appendices
NIEURLET	16/6/18		In hospital 2/Lieut. T.D. Stock.	
	17/6/18		40th Div Order 84H (Q) Received	
	18/6/18		119th Infantry Brigade Operation Order No 10. Received	
			Do No 11. Received	
	19/6/18		119th Infantry Brigade letter 724/9.L. Received	
			Carried on with Battalion training	
	20/6/18		Do	
	21/6/18		Do	
	22/6/18		2/Lieut A.H. BAKER. Transferred to 40th Div. Recp Camp - Struck off strength	
			119th Infantry Brigade Operation order No 12 - Received	
	23/6/18	7.30 am	Battalion moved off from NIEURLET by duckboard track to ST. OMER & entrain.	
ST. OMER		9.30 am	Battalion entrained.	
Shut 27.8 U.7 C.7.8.		12 noon	Arrived camp near HAZEBROUCK	
	24/6/18		119th Infantry Brigade letter 83/S/G. Received.	
	25/6/18		Do Letter 10/6/G. Received.	

WAR DIARY
or
INTELLIGENCE SUMMARY.

(Erase heading not required.)

Army Form C. 2118.

Place	Date	Hour	Summary of Events and Information	Remarks and references to Appendices
Sheet 29. U.17.c.7.8.	25/6/18	9.10am	Telegram from 119th Inf. Bde. "Practice EVEN NOW"	
		10 am	Battalion moved up to line.	
		1.30 pm	Trenches, garrisons and outposts completed.	
		4 pm	Return to billets	
			119th Infantry Brigade Operation Order No 13. Received.	
	26/6/18		Carried on with Battalion training	
	27/6/18		do	
	28/6/18		do	
	29/6/18		do	
	30/6/18		Defence Scheme Arpaen - WEST HAZEBROUCK LINE - (Copy attached).	
			Carried on with Battalion training.	

Sheridan Kilpsan
Lt. Col.
Comdg. 13th Bn. Roy. Irish Rifles

SECRET.   13th R. Innis Fus.   COPY

DEFENCE SCHEME

Map ref. Sheet 27 S.E.
Western Half, Edition 2d Local
1/20.000.

1. In the event of an enemy attack on the Second Army Front, 110th Inf Bde & attached troops will man the West Hazebrouck Line, the Southern boundary being V.21.b.9.0 - 15.c.5.7 - 14.b.6.0 - a.o.o. and Northern boundary being W.7.b.37 - V.2.b.5.0.9.0. 6.c.6.5 - 5 Central.

2. The Brigade section will be held with two battns in main line of resistance and observation line, the 13th Royal Inniskilling Fusiliers on the right, and 13th East Lancashire Regt. on the left, dividing line between battns. being BORRE - BECQUE (inclusive to left Battn) V.11.c.4.4 - 10 Centre, on the right of the 13th Roy. Innis. Fus will be the 3rd Bn. Cheshire Regt.

3. DISTRIBUTION. The line of resistance with the battn, with outposts, will be held by G Coy (+75 Lab. Corps) on the right, and H Coy (+70 Lab. Corps) on the left, dividing line being track from V.16.d.3.6. to Bn. H.Q.
   No withdrawal from the line of Resistance without orders from Commanding Officer.

4. The outpost line will consist of a chain of strong points located as follows:-

   No. 1. V.21.b.8.0.   30 O.R. Lewis Gun ⎫ G Coy
   " 2. V.22.a.4.2.   30 O.R.   ⎬ 1 officer
   " 3. V.22.a.6.4.   30. O.R.   ⎭
   " 4. V.22.b.05.-6.0.   30 O.R. Lewis Gun ⎱ G Coy
   " 5. V.22.b.9.5.   30 O.R. Lewis Gun ⎰
   " 6. V.23.a.8.4.   30 O.R.   ⎫ H Coy
   " 7. V.23.b.3.5.-6.5. 30 O.R. Lewis Gun ⎬ 1 officer

Intermediate posts will be established at:-

No 1	V.21.b.5.4	25 O.R.	}	G. Coy.
" 2	V.22.a.4.8	25 O.R.	}	1 Officer
" 3	V.22.b.1.5-9.5	25 O.R.	}	
" 4	V.16.d.7.5.-1.5	25 O.R.	}	
" 5	V.17.c.1.5.-4.5	25 O.R.	}	H Coy.
" 6	V.17.a.3.0.-6.5	25 O.R.	}	1 Officer.
" 7	V.17.a.8.9.	25 O.R.	}	

2 Coys. and balance of Labour Corps attached, in reserve near Battn. H.Q.

5. Battn. H.Q. in farm at V.10.c.8.2.
   ~~Right Front Coy. in house at V.15.c.9.7.~~
   Left Front Coy. in farm at V.16.c.9.4.
   Battn. aid post in farm at V.10.c.7.5.

6. Communication between outpost and intermediate lines with line of resistance by visual and runners. Between Bn. H.Q. & Front Line Coys. by telephone visual and runners.

7. In the event of an attack by the enemy, the outpost line will, ~~if possible~~ stop his advance, ~~at least delay his advance to the last possible moment before withdrawing on intermediate line, trusting endeavour should be made to~~ The intermediate line will hold the enemy. Should the enemy succeed in driving ~~in our advanced~~ troops and gain a footing in our line of resistance a counter attack will at once be made.

8. GAS. In the event of the enemy using gas or gas shelling, respirators will at once be put on, but sentries must keep on the alert to detect any advancing troops, on whom a steady fire would be maintained.

9. Slightly wounded men will not leave the trenches during an attack, but be attended to by stretcher bearers in the trench.

On no account will men other than stretcher bearers bring wounded to the rear during an attack.

(Sgd) J. Plunkett Lt.Col.
Comdg. 13th R. Innis. Fus.

29.6.18

WAR DIARY
INTELLIGENCE SUMMARY

13 R Sussex — Army Form C. 2118.
Vol 2

Place	Date	Hour	Summary of Events and Information	Remarks and references to Appendices
Sheet 27 U.17.c.7.8	1/7/18		Carried on Battalion training	
		Nd. of NW butts	Battalion will supply EAST HAZEBROUCK LINE from 3/7/18 to 6/7/18 inclusive to instruct men in trench duties	
	2/7/18		Inspected by H.R.H. Duke of Connaught	
	3/7/18	9.30 a.m.	Battalion moved off by march route to man EAST HAZEBROUCK LINE	
V.15.a.9.1			Battalion H.Q. in EAST HAZEBROUCK LINE - tents. 4 Companies in trenches	
	4/7/18		Carried on with trench training - working parties - No happening of any importance	
	5/7/18		Inter-Company relief carried out	
	6/7/18		Carried on with instruction in trench duties under instructors from 9th Division	
	7/7/18		Battalion relieved in EAST HAZEBROUCK LINE by 13th EAST LANCASHIRE REGT.	
U.17.c.9.8	8/7/18		Carried on with Battalion training	
			Station Staff Officers order received (Buzancy)	
	9/7/18		Carried on with Battalion training	
	10/7/18		Carried on with Battalion training	
	11/7/18		Carried on with Battalion training	

WAR DIARY
or
INTELLIGENCE SUMMARY.
(Erase heading not required.)

Army Form C. 2118.

Place	Date	Hour	Summary of Events and Information	Remarks and references to Appendices
U17c9.8	13/7/18		Carried on Battalion training	
	14/7/18		Operation order No 4 issued	Op Sheet 2/1 dated 14/7/18
			1. A practice manning of the trenches in the N sector of the W. HAZEBROUCK LINE will be carried out by 119th Inf Bde and affiliated about RE Coys on nights 15th July.	
			2. The Bn with attached about Coys will man the right Sector of the Bn front in accordance with the Scheme already issued will be carried out by 9.30am.	
			The Bn will move off in the following order — C H.Q. of G Coy & H.Q. details	
			G Coy will move off at 6.00 am and will pass V 7 d 8 1 at 7.15 am.	
			Route V13 6 8 9 V15 a 3 5.	
			3. 1 Limber will accompany each Coy with its Lewis Guns, Limber carrying 21 boxes SAA & 12 picks and spades and each carrying 2 Boxes SAA will accompany each of G & H Coys	
			4. Personnel will be left behind in accordance with attached request. Coy C.S.M. Reeve will be in charge of that party and will report to the Adjutant at 9am. This personnel will enclose the coys to be left behind in charge of tents clothes etc.	

WAR DIARY
or
INTELLIGENCE SUMMARY.

Army Form C. 2118.

Place	Date	Hour	Summary of Events and Information	Remarks and references to Appendices
U.17.c.9.8.	14/7/18		Operation Order No 4	
			5. 1 Section of 19th T.M.B. will be attached to the batteries. This section will join the Bn at V.13.c.36. & will move to rear of HQ. Details	
			wheelers will report to HQ 119th T.M.B. at 6.30 am. 14th Section will report to the adjutant for instructions on	
			arrival at 119 Bn H.Q. at V.10.c.8.2.	
			6. The Watson will be at V.11.a.5.5. at 9.30 am tomorrow &	
			will Labour (G) and Command them from 119 T.M.B.	
			7. I (G) will detail 1/Cpl & 4 men to be attached for the day	
			to T.M.B. This party will report to 119 T.M.B. at 6.45 am.	
			8. Balance of Transport as proceeding to the line will	
			concentrate at U.7.b.	
			9. Coys Three details by H.Q.(G) for strengths &	
			will report to present Bn H.Q. V.13.c.6 at 7 pm	
			to-morrow.	

WAR DIARY or INTELLIGENCE SUMMARY

Army Form C. 2118.

(Erase heading not required.)

Instructions regarding War Diaries and Intelligence Summaries are contained in F. S. Regs., Part II. and the Staff Manual respectively. Title pages will be prepared in manuscript.

Place	Date	Hour	Summary of Events and Information	Remarks and references to Appendices
Sheet 27 U.17.c.9.8.	15/9/18		Battalion occupied N Sector of N HAZEBROUCK LINE	
	16/9/18		Carried on Battalion Training. Operation Order No 15 issued.	
	16/9/18		119th Inf Bde. Operation order No 5 issued.	Reference Sheet 27 1/20000 Sheet 27 NE 1/10000 Sheet 36a NE 1/20000
			1. The 119th Inf Bde will relieve the 83rd Inf Bde on the line S.W. of MERRIS on 17/18th July	
			2. The Battn will move to-morrow to BC lines in E.1.	
			H.Q. details will move off at 8 am followed by G.H.I of Coy	
			H.Q. details will pass starting point V.19.c.9.5 at 8.50 am	
			Route U.18.d.36 – V.19.c.9.5 – V.20.a.6.2 – V.21.a.5.4 – V.23.a.5.8 – V.23.d.1.6 – V.23.d.8.8 – V.24.c.9.5 – E.1.C.8.1. Brass fighting wear	
			Unconsumed portion of days ration to be taken on the man	
			200x distance between Platoons. Less sec'n leaders will follow on under Sgt Drummond	

WAR DIARY
or
INTELLIGENCE SUMMARY.
(Erase heading not required.)

Army Form C. 2118.

Place	Date	Hour	Summary of Events and Information	Remarks and references to Appendices
U.17.c.9.5	16/7/18		Operation order N° 5 (contd)	
			3. On arrival in New area the Batts will form under the orders	
			of 87th Inf Bde (H.Q. W.25.a.58)	
			4. Personnel of 119th Signalling School at 13th Bombing School will not	
			accompany units. They will take over tents vacated by T.M.B.	
			5. Baggage in accordance with details named will be left behind	
			and will proceed to the new Transport lines under the Transport	
			Officer	
			6. Transport lines & QM Stores will be at V.20.a.59.	
			Separate instructions will be issued to Transport Officer	
			7. The Bn will remain under 40 Division formation moves	
			service. Rations for consumption 19th July will be	
			delivered to new transport lines. N° 2 Coy 40 Division	
			train in standcamp at STAPLE.	
			8. Yr I of Coy will each detail an N.C.O. & five men	
			to be a Guard over tents & shelters in present area.	
			The 87th Inf Bde will use this accommodation as required during	
			the relief	

WAR DIARY
or
INTELLIGENCE SUMMARY.
(Erase heading not required.)

Army Form C. 2118.

Place	Date	Hour	Summary of Events and Information	Remarks and references to Appendices
41 c 9.8.	16/7/18		Operation Order No 5. (contd) 9. Pass Blanks with identifying names will be obtained by C/O at Assembly billets. Blankets to be in bundles of ten (10). These will be conveyed to mens Transport lines under arrangements to be made by Transport Officer. Officers' Kits and Officers mess Kits (1 trestle (a)) both at Q.M. Stores by 7 am. 10. The greatest of present in the Ammunition and Water Dumps will remain and must be reported by Both. 11. The greatest care is to be taken that the A&E Camp is left in a scrupulously clean condition. 12. The Battalion will move to the forming line on the 18/7/18 under orders of the 87th Inf Bde.	
	17/7/16		1st Border Regt Operation order No 16 received. Battalion occupied B & C lines. BN HQ at W.25	

WAR DIARY
or
INTELLIGENCE SUMMARY.

Army Form C. 2118.

Place	Date	Hour	Summary of Events and Information	Remarks and references to Appendices
W 25	18/1/18		Operation order No 6 issued	Ref. map STAZEELE 1/20000
			1. The batn will relieve the 1st Bn Bedford Regt in the line on night 18/19th July as follows:-	
			A Coy Bedford Regt on right front line by E Coy of this Bn	
			B " " " left " " " H " " "	
			2 right platoons " " " " I " " "	
			D Coy " " " in support line	
			2 left platoons " " " " J " " "	
			2. Guides have already been attached from 1st Bedford Regt	
			Coys of this Bn proceeding	
			3. Before taking over reliefs lists of gas alerts, trench stores SAA Grenades, Emergency rations will be carefully checked	
			Return of same in hand and proposed work ahead to be taken over	
			Copy of last of stores taken over and expected growth to reach the Adjutant by 9 am on 19th inst.	

Army Form C. 2118.

WAR DIARY
or
INTELLIGENCE SUMMARY.
(Erase heading not required.)

Instructions regarding War Diaries and Intelligence Summaries are contained in F.S. Regs., Part II. and the Staff Manual respectively. Title pages will be prepared in manuscript.

Place	Date	Hour	Summary of Events and Information	Remarks and references to Appendices
W.25.	18/7/18		Operation order No 6 (Contd) 4. On completion of relief Coys will work with Bn. H.Q. by Coys work "VETERANS"	
			5. Trenches in front are to be thoroughly cleaned before vacating.	
			6. Acknowledge.	
			Battalion moved off in autobuses to relief of 1st Border Regt.	
			Relief completed.	
Pill's House E.6.a.9.9.	19/7/18		Half an hour after relief 2 prisoners were brought in by H.Q.	
			Casualties 5 O.R. killed 4 O.R. wounded	
			Defence scheme received. Support plus Reserve front	
			13th E. Lancs Regt.	Ref. Map Sheet 27 1/40,000 Steen-Werken sheet 28 N.E. 1/20,000 36a N.E.
	20/7/18		Operation Order No 7 issued.	
			1. An inter-company relief will take place with night of 20/21st July.	
			Front line. C Coy will be relieved by I Coy. H.	
			Support D Coy will move into positions occupied by I Coy	

WAR DIARY
or
INTELLIGENCE SUMMARY.

(Erase heading not required.)

Army Form C. 2118.

Place	Date	Hour	Summary of Events and Information	Remarks and references to Appendices
TIFLIS HOUSE E.5.a.0.9.	20/1/18		Operation Order No 7 (contd) 2. I/9 Coy will not move from their present positions before 10.30 pm. 3. Guides from C Coy for I Coy will meet 9 Coy H.Q. at 10.30 pm and Guides from H Coy for J Coy & J Coy H.Q. at 10.15 pm. Guides to be on platoon scale. 4. Trench stores will be taken over by relieving Coy and receipts in duplicate to be sent to Battalions H.Q. the Adjutant keeping one. 27/1/18 5. Completion of relief will be notified to the Adjutant by the Coy by the Code word "RANGE". 6. Separate instructions will be issued as regards rations, water & hot food. 7. Acknowledge. Inter-Company relief carried out	
	20/1/18		119th Inf Bde Operation Order No 11 received Provisional Defence Scheme received	

WAR DIARY
or
INTELLIGENCE SUMMARY.
(Erase heading not required.)

Army Form C. 2118.

Place	Date	Hour	Summary of Events and Information	Remarks and references to Appendices
TIFLIS HOUSE E.S.6.0.9.	21/9/18		Operation Order No 8 issued:—	
			R/sheet 27 S.E. Western Half. Edition 4. Local Sheet 36 N.E. 1/20,000	
			1. The battⁿ will be relieved on night 22/23 inst as follows	
			Front Line A Coy E Lancs Regt will relieve T Coy R Innis Fus. on the right	
			D ,, ,, ,, ,, ,, ,, left	
			Support B ,, ,, ,, ,, ,, ,, right	
			C ,, ,, ,, ,, ,, ,, left	
			2. T Coy will have one guide per Platoon at Front Line Regt Coy H.Q. at 10.15 p.m.	
			,, ,, ,, ,, ,, ,, Bn. H.Q. at 10.15 p.m.	
			G & H Coys will each have one guide per Coy at Bn. H.Q. at 11.15 p.m.	
			3. Advance parties of E. Lancs are reporting at Coy H.Q. tonight, 1 N.C.O. will be accommodated in each post and one trench r-	
			area stores etc. will be checked in daylight tomorrow.	
			Trench area stores which include food containers water tins	
			will be handed over to relieving Coy and a consolidated list	
			for the whole Coy, signed by O.C. both Coys (or a duplicate) will be	
			handed to the Adjutant by 9am on 23rd instant	

WAR DIARY
or
INTELLIGENCE SUMMARY.
(Erase heading not required.)

Army Form C. 2118.

Place	Date	Hour	Summary of Events and Information	Remarks and references to Appendices
TIFLIS HOUSE E.5.a.0.9	21/11/18		Operation Order No 8 (contd) Receipts by posts will not be accepted. R.S.M. will hand over payments, all Receipts from Qr. Mr. at Coy HQ. at 7pm 22nd inst. and the Quartermaster will hand over all Trench Stores at Transport Lines. Checking in all cases must be carefully done.	
			4. Work Parties in hand will also be handed over to relieving Coy.	
			5. While relief is in progress 1 of Coy will pass post covering relief. These patrols will remain out until relieved by patrols of E Lancs.	
			6. T Coy will detail 1 Sgt. to remain at N° 3 post of Coy 1 Sgt. to remain at N°4 Post for 24 hours after relief. Name of Sgt. to be notified to transport by Coy Commanders.	
			6a. Completion of relief to be notified by Code word "ROD"	

WAR DIARY
or
INTELLIGENCE SUMMARY.
(Erase heading not required.)

Army Form C. 2118.

Place	Date	Hour	Summary of Events and Information	Remarks and references to Appendices
TIFLIS HOUSE E.5.a.9.	24/7/16		Operation order 709 (contd) 7. On completion of relief Bn will move into Reserve at V24 taking over from 12th N. Staffs. Platoons will move to their billets independently. Advance parties of Officers & N.C.O's for B will report to O/C Regiment at 11 am to move for the purpose of reconnoitring billets. The advance officer for B will arrange for guides to meet his platoon at x Roads V24 c-95 25. 8. Transport officer & Q.M. Stores will remain at present location. 9. The Quartermaster will be responsible for arranging that the men's packs and blankets are moved to the new area and also, a suitable Guard over. Also they will arrange so that they can be properly distributed to the men. He will also be responsible for seeing that officers kits and mess kits are moved to new area. 10. Quartermaster will arrange for all cooking to be done & men's billets and will have a hot meal ready for the men to-morrow night.	

WAR DIARY or INTELLIGENCE SUMMARY

Army Form C. 2118.

Place	Date	Hour	Summary of Events and Information	Remarks and references to Appendices
TIFLIS HOUSE E.S.a.O.q.	21/9/18	11	Operation order No 8 (copy) 1 Limber for HQ officers kits 1 limber for Orderly Room and 1 Limber for HQ mess kits 1 mess kits will be at Bn HQ 10pm. Signalling Sgt will be at Bn HQ 10pm. G+H Coy limbers will report at Bn HQ at 12 midnight. I + J (Coy) limbers will leave 'O' in MONT DE MERRIS E5C53 (Ration dump) at 7pm. Coys are responsible that limbers are properly loaded up. A FACS mule will report to ad post for Medical Equipment etc at 11pm.	
		12	Reconnoitrage. Casualties - Lt C.H. HICKS - Killed. 2/Lt R WATSON - WOUNDED. 1 OR killed 5 OR wounded 5 OR missing.	
	22/9/18		Out post line garrisoned. Casualties. Capt C.V.E. CAREW - wounded. 1 OR killed 6 OR wounded 1 OR missing. Battalion relieved in front line by 13th E. LANCS. REGT.	
V24 d 4.8	23/9/18		Battalion moved to reserve line at Bn HQ V24 d 4.8.	

WAR DIARY or INTELLIGENCE SUMMARY

Army Form C. 2118.

Place	Date	Hour	Summary of Events and Information	Remarks and references to Appendices
V 20 d 10 8	24/7/18		General clean up. Working parties, supplies.	
	25/7/18		Working parties	
	26/7/18		Working parties	
			Operation order No. 9 issued. Ref. 27 S.E. WESTERN & EASTERN Antwerp Edition 4th Local 36a IV S.E. 1/20,000	
			1. The battalion will relieve 12th I.Y. STAFFS in outpost on the 119th Inf. Bde.
			Relief on the night of 26/27th 1918 as follows:-
			C Coy 13th Rhondda Bns will relieve A Coy 12 I.Y. Staffs in right support
			H " " " " C " " " left "
			I " " " " B " " " right reserve
			J " " " " D " " " left "
			2. Companies will move independently by platoons.
			H.Q. details will move at 2-10 p.m. under Lt. & Adjutant followed by C.H.I. of J. Roys. Right Coy will proceed by KELT CROSSING, and Left Coy by TRADELLES.
			Further details and arrangements as to Guides to be made.
			O.C's Coys concerned

WAR DIARY
INTELLIGENCE SUMMARY

Army Form C. 2118.

Place	Date	Hour	Summary of Events and Information	Remarks and references to Appendices
V.24.d.4.8.	26/7/18		Operation order No 9 (contd) 3. Before taking over lots of part photo trench stores S.A.A. grenades Emergency rations etc. will be carefully checked.	
			A consolidated receipt for the whole store taken over by C/Os will be made out and signed in duplicate and one copy will be handed to the Adjutant by 9 am. 27/7/18	
			R.S.M. will take over stores etc. at Bn H.Q. 8.30 pm. tonight	
			4. On completion of relief C/Os will notify Bn HQ at CURZON HOUSE (F.3.c.1.7) by one word "feed"	
			5. Separate instructions have been issued to Transport Officer and Quartermaster. Lewis Guns will accompany Coys. L.G. Lambert	
			6. Present billets to be left clean and tidy and a Certificate to that effect will be rendered to Adjutant by 9.30 pm. tonight	
	26/7/18		119th Inf Bde S.M. 113 received Battalion relieved 125th Staffs in support line.	

WAR DIARY
or
INTELLIGENCE SUMMARY.
(Erase heading not required.)

Army Form C. 2118.

Place	Date	Hour	Summary of Events and Information	Remarks and references to Appendices
E.3.c.1.7.	27/7/16		Battalion H.Q. established at CURFEW HOUSE	
	28/7/16		Carried on with building parapets - Working parties supplies	
	29/7/16		Carried on with building parapets - Working parties supplies	
			119th Inf. Bde Operation Order No. 19 received	
	30/7/16		Operation Order No. 10 - issued	
			Ref. Sheet 27 S.E. 4° scale. WESTERN HALF 1/20.000	
			36a N.E. 1/20.000	
			27 + 36a 1/40.000	
			1. The 19th R.Inf. Fus. will be relieved by the 12th & Inf. Btn. on 30 July - 1st August	
			2. The batn. will be relieved by the 23rd R. James Fus. on night of	
			31st July/1st Aug as follows:-	
			B Coy 23rd James Fus. will relieve C 19th R Inf Fus on right support	
			C " " " " " H " " " left "	
			D " " " " " I " " " right reserve	
			A " " " " " J " " " left "	
			There will be no movement forward of Reserve Line before 9.30 p.m.	

WAR DIARY
or
INTELLIGENCE SUMMARY.

Army Form C. 2118.

Place	Date	Hour	Summary of Events and Information	Remarks and references to Appendices
E.3.c.1.7.	30.7.18		Operation Order No. 10 (contd) 3. Each Coy will send one guide to Platoon & Sect	
			for Coy H.Q. to report to 2nd Lt. W.W. MARTIN at Pn. 118.	
			CURFEW HOUSE at 8.15.p.m. They will proceed under	
			2ND LT. W.W. MARTIN to road junction BORRE. (W.19.C.95.70.)	
			4. Advance party of 1 Officer and 4 N.C.O's per Coy are being	
			sent to-day by 23rd LANCS. FUS. to be attached to Coys.	
			5. All present maps, Sketches, plans of work and defence	
			schemes will be handed over separately and receipts	
			taken from officer of advance party. Receipt to be handed	
			to Adjutant by 8pm. 31/7/18	
			6. Trench and area stores will be handed over to Officer i/c	
			Advance party in accordance with forpormas	
			issued to Coys. The receipts will be made out in	
			duplicate and one copy will be handed to Adjutant by 8/pm.	
			31/7/18. Coys will also obtain the signature of Officer i/c	
			Advance party to the certificate that trench etc,	

A6945 Wt. W1142/M1160 350,000 12/16 D. D. & L. Forms/C./2118/14

WAR DIARY
or
INTELLIGENCE SUMMARY.

(Erase heading not required.)

Army Form C. 2118.

Place	Date	Hour	Summary of Events and Information	Remarks and references to Appendices
E.3.c.1.7.	30/7/18		Operation Order No 10 (Ops) Q	

Operation Order No 10 (Ops) Q

has been handed over in a clean and sanitary condition.

Greatcoats to be taken that everything that was taken over by the Loyal North Lancs are to relieving Bn. Respective that have been sent up from Q.M. Stores not which are not to be handed over. They will be carefully collected and placed at the Coy Ration dump where they will be looked on lorries. R.S.M. will hand over all stores at Bn. H.Q. Q.M. will hand over all ambulance Stores at Transport lines. He will forward the receipt and above certificate that the Transport Lines have been handed over in a clean and sanitary condition to this Regulator by 5 p.m. 31/7/18

7. Loyo will also obtain & forward to the Adjutant by 3 p.m. 31/7/18 a certificate that all equipment in handed over in clean & sanitary condition.

8. All guides with duties in hand will be handed over to relieving Coys.

WAR DIARY
or
INTELLIGENCE SUMMARY.
(Erase heading not required.)

Army Form C. 2118.

Place	Date	Hour	Summary of Events and Information	Remarks and references to Appendices
E.3.c.17.	30/1/18		Operation order no 10 (contd) 9. Completion of relief to be notified to Bn Hd by code word "CLUB".	
		10.	Transport officer will have one limber (covered in) and another limber for water cans, camp kettles etc., at Bn HQ. Accomp at 10.7pm 31/7/18. He will also have at 12 m. HQ. at 10.7pm the Mess Cart & limber. Reserve for C.O., Capt White, and the Adjutant will be at ONWARD CROSSING (V.24.a.9.7) at 12 midnight.	
		11.	On relief the Bn will move to former camp at U.17. Coys will move independently with Coy Hd distance between platoons. Rent- L'HOFFAND - V.22.d.1.0 - V.20.d.6.2. - LES CINQ RUES.	
		12.	Advance parties of 1 officer and 1 N.C.O per Coy will report to A/Adjutant at moment to-morrow at Bn HQ. They will proceed to camp at U.17 and prepare the camp	

WAR DIARY
or
INTELLIGENCE SUMMARY.

Army Form C. 2118.

Place	Date	Hour	Summary of Events and Information	Remarks and references to Appendices
E.3.c.17.	30/7/18		Operation Order No 10 (Cont'd) 13) The Q.M. will take over camp at V.17 from E. LANCS	
			He will have the men's packs dumped at the Coy (camping ground) would have to ready for the men on arrival.	
			14) Acknowledge.	
	30/7/18		Casualties 10 R.Killed 1 O.R. wounded 2 O.R. Gassed	
U.17.	31/7/18		Battalion relieved by 23rd Lancs. Fus. Battalion arrived in camp. Tents & shelters.	
			31/7/18	
			[signed] Stanley Kilburne Major Commanding 1st/4th Roy. Lancaster Regt.	

Confidential

War Diary of 13th Bn. Royal Inniskilling Fusiliers

From 1/8/1918 To 31/8/1918

(VOLUME 1)

Army Form C. 2118.

WAR DIARY
or
INTELLIGENCE SUMMARY.
(Erase heading not required.)

Instructions regarding War Diaries and Intelligence Summaries are contained in F. S. Regs., Part II. and the Staff Manual respectively. Title pages will be prepared in manuscript.

Place	Date	Hour	Summary of Events and Information	Remarks and references to Appendices
Sheet 27				
U.7.c.7.8	1/8/18		Battalion arrived in camp after relief in line.	
"	2/8/18		Carried on Battalion training	
"	3/8/18		Carried on battalion training	
"	4/8/18		Carried on battalion training. 6 O.R. reported for duty	
"	5/8/18		Carried on battalion training. MAJOR E.R. O'CONNOR joined for duty	
"	6/8/18		Carried on battalion training	
"	7/8/18		Carried on battalion training	
"	8/8/18		Carried on battalion training - 2/Lt A.S. WILSON joined for duty.	
"	9/8/18		Carried on battalion training	
"	10/8/18		Carried on battalion training - Battalion Sports	
"	11/8/18		Carried on battalion training	
"	12/8/18		Carried on battalion training	
"	13/8/18		Carried on battalion training - 2/Lt H.E. McMAHON jones for duty	
"	14/8/18		Carried on battalion training - 119th Inf. Bde operation order No. 18 received	
"	15/8/18		Carried on battalion training	
"	16/8/18		Carried on battalion training	

WAR DIARY
or
INTELLIGENCE SUMMARY

Army Form C. 2118.

(Erase heading not required.)

Place	Date	Hour	Summary of Events and Information	Remarks and references to Appendices
Sheet 27 U.17.c.78	6.8.18		Operation order No.11 issued. Ref Map 1/20000. 27 SE (WESTERN HALF (4th Edit))	
			1. Instructions regarding occupation of WEST HAZEBROUCK LINE are cancelled and following substitute.	
			2. In the event of an enemy attack on the 2nd Army front the 119th Infantry Brigade will man the WEST HAZEBROUCK LINE	
			N. Boundary. W.7.a.1.1. – V.12.c.50.95 along road to P.35.c.6.1. – P.35.c.6.50. – P.33.a.6.0	
			S. Boundary WALLON CAPPEL along the gare line to U.30.c.19. – U.30.c.86. – V.25.a.88. – V.26.a.0.8. – V.26 central	
			The Brigade Section will be held by the 12th Bn. NORTH STAFFS REGT. on the right, and the 13th Bn. ROY. INNIS. FUS. on the left, both battns having attached troops.	
			Dividing line between Battns V.22.c.21. – V.16.c.90. – V.16.a.27. – V.12.c.0.0	
			Major BELLAMY'S Battn will be on the left of the 13th R. INNIS. F-45.	

WAR DIARY
or
INTELLIGENCE SUMMARY.
(Erase heading not required.)

Army Form C. 2118.

Place	Date	Hour	Summary of Events and Information	Remarks and references to Appendices
Sheet 27				
V.17.c.7.8	16/8/18		Operation N° 11 Contd. 3. Distribution. Z Line, Outpost & Intermediate Lines will be held by 'C' Coy on the right, 'H' Coy in the centre and 'I' Coy on the left. Dividing lines being V.18.a.7.2 — V.11.b.6.0 and V.23.b.7.0 — V.10.d.9.0.	
			OUTPOST LINE — a chain of posts as follows:—	
			N° 1 at V.22 central . . . . . . 30 O.R. Lewis Gun. ⎫	
			" 2 . V.22.b.6.4 . . . . . . 30 O.R. ⎬ G Coy	
			" 3 . V.22.b.9.5 . . . . . . 30 O.R. Lewis Gun ⎭	
			" 4 . V.23.a.8.4 . . . . . . 30 O.R.	
			" 5 . V.23.b.35.65 . . . . . . 30 O.R. Lewis Gun ⎫	
			" 6 . V.18.c.1.4 . . . . . . 30 O.R. ⎬ H Coy	
			" 7 . V.18.d.1.6 . . . . . . 30 O.R. Lewis Gun ⎭	
			" 8 . V.18.b.9.3 . . . . . . 30 O.R. ⎫ I Coy	
			" 9 . W.7.c.6.4. . . . . . . 30 O.R. Lewis Gun ⎭	

WAR DIARY
or
INTELLIGENCE SUMMARY.
(Erase heading not required.)

Army Form C. 2118.

Place	Date	Hour	Summary of Events and Information	Remarks and references to Appendices
Sheet 27 U.17.c.7.8.	16/8/18		Operation Order No.11 contd. 3 INTERMEDIATE LINE. A chain of posts as follows:-	
			N°1 at V.22.b.15.95. 30 OR Lewis Gun ⎫	
			„ 2 „ V.16.d.95.15. 30 OR „ „ ⎬ G.Coy	
			„ 3 „ V.17.c.15.45. 30 OR Lewis Gun ⎭	
			„ 4 „ V.17.d.30.65. 30 OR ⎫	
			„ 5 „ V.17.a.8.9. 30 OR ⎬ H.Coy	
			„ 6 „ V.18.a.4.2. 30 OR Lewis Gun ⎭	
			„ 7 „ V.18.b.1.8. 30 OR ⎫	
			„ 8 „ V.12.d.8.3. 30 OR ⎬ I.Coy	
			„ 9 „ V.13.c.1.9. 30 OR Lewis Gun ⎭	
			J.Coy in reserve near Bn. HQ.	
			Labour troops distribution as follows:-	
			attached to G.Coy. 210 of 6th Labour Coy	
			„ „ H „ 150 13th „	
			„ „ I „ 150 132nd „	
			Bn. HQ. N° 188 Labour Coy + balance of 6th 13th & 132nd Labour Coys about 646 OR in all.	

WAR DIARY
or
INTELLIGENCE SUMMARY.

(Erase heading not required.)

Army Form C. 2118.

Place	Date	Hour	Summary of Events and Information	Remarks and references to Appendices
Sheet 27 U.7.c.7.8.	16/8/16		Operation order No 11 (contd) 4. No withdrawal from any line without orders from the Group officer.	
		5	WARNING. On receipt of Code word - "EVENOW" Coys will move as early as possible and take up positions in accordance with scheme taking any route N of Line V.13 central - to central	
			Labour Coys for 13th R. Inns. Div. assemble at bivouacs at V.10.a.5.4 and V.10.a.3.1.	
			An officer from each Coy on arrival will proceed to V.10.a.4.2 and receive over the requisite number of Labour Coys and conduct them to respective HQ.	
		6	Bn HQ at Farm V.5.c.6.3	
			"Aid Post - "	
			Reserve Coy - "	
			Right Front Coy - V.10.a.8.1	
			Centre - " - V.11.d.5.3	
			Left - " - V.6.c.4.0	

WAR DIARY
or
INTELLIGENCE SUMMARY.
(Erase heading not required.)

Army Form C. 2118.

Place	Date	Hour	Summary of Events and Information	Remarks and references to Appendices
Sheet 27 U.17 c. 7.8	16/8/18		Operation Order No 11 (contd) 7. Communication between Outpost & Intermediate lines with Z line by visual runners, between Coy H.Q and Bn H.Q by telephone, visual runners. 8. In the event of the enemy using Gas or Gas shelling, respirators will at once be put on, but sentries must keep on the alert to detect any advancing enemy troops on whom a steady fire would be maintained. 9. Slightly wounded men will not leave their posts during an attack but be attended to by stretcher bearers present. On no account will other than stretcher bearers bring wounded to the rear during an attack. 10. Administrative Instructions. (i) Dress. Fighting Order. (ii) Tents Supplies Kits 2/5. (a) Tents & shelters will be struck and dumped with Surplus kit next the road ready for loading	

WAR DIARY
or
INTELLIGENCE SUMMARY

Army Form C. 2118.

Place	Date	Hour	Summary of Events and Information	Remarks and references to Appendices
Sheet 27 U.1 C.7.8	16/9/8		Operation Order No 11 (Contd)	
			(i) 2/L. Parry with 3 OR each from G.H.Q. and S.O.R. each from I.T.y. Coys will be detailed to guard the Battalion dump. They will be provided with 3 days rations.	
			(b) As many kits etc. as possible will be sent to RENESCURE on 1st line transport. EMPTY ammunition and ration limbers returning from the line will collect as many as possible.	
			(ii) Transport.	
			(a) Immediately on receipt of code word "ENENOW" all transport other than that proceeding with S.A.A. will be sent to T.22.a.6. (South of the Railway) (near RENESCURE).	
			(b) The transport limbers for the line will also proceed to T.22.a.6 as soon as no longer required.	
			(c) L. Stamming, 3rd E. Lan. Regt. will be in charge. All transport of No 8 Inf. Bde. On arrival at this new base will be under his control.	

WAR DIARY
or
INTELLIGENCE SUMMARY.

Army Form C. 2118.

Place	Date	Hour	Summary of Events and Information	Remarks and references to Appendices
Sheet 27 U.17.c.7.8	16/8/18		Operation Order No.11 (contd.) 19 (iii) (c) Detail 2 mounted orderlies per batt with rations & forage to report to Bde HQ to act as liaison	
			IV Rations	
			(a) Unconsumed portion of pack rations and iron ration will be taken on the man	
			(b) From the day following the occupation of the line rations will be delivered to Transport Lines in T.22 a. & 6 by MT Lorry	
			40 Divn Train	
			(c) Units attached Limber Waters will be rationed by it batn utilizes to the best advantage. The transport of these units being packed with the Bn Transport	
			(d) A.B.S.S. on the day of occupation of the line will unload the figures for all attached units and rations will on the following day to Bn transport lines will be in accordance with these figures	

Army Form C. 2118.

WAR DIARY
or
INTELLIGENCE SUMMARY.
(Erase heading not required.)

Instructions regarding War Diaries and Intelligence Summaries are contained in F. S. Regs., Part II. and the Staff Manual respectively. Title pages will be prepared in manuscript.

Place	Date	Hour	Summary of Events and Information	Remarks and references to Appendices
Sheet 27				
U.17.c.7.8.	19/4/18		Operation order No.11 (contd 10.1V.18). The Q.M.S. of each attached unit will be attached to Coy	
			as necessary with the Q.M. of the Bn.	
			9. Q.M. will notify Bn. HQ. by 4-0 pm daily units Ration	
			Requirements, ack rations etc	
			10. Water.	
			(a) Forward water points	
			V.7.d.6.1. U.17.a.0.0. V.4.c.3.0.	
			Rendezvous point to transport lines U.19.c.59. Ebblinghem	
			(b) Back area water points	
			WALLON CAPPEL V.28.6.8.7.	
			LYNDE B.6.d.5.8.	
			BLARINGHEM B.23.b.1.4.	
			PONT ASQUIN B.8.a.7.9.	
			WARDRECQUES A.12.a.3.2.	
			RACQUINGHEM A.13.a.9.3.	
			RENESCURE T.20.d.6.8.	

Army Form C. 2118.

WAR DIARY
or
INTELLIGENCE SUMMARY.
(Erase heading not required.)

Instructions regarding War Diaries and Intelligence Summaries are contained in F. S. Regs., Part II. and the Staff Manual respectively. Title pages will be prepared in manuscript.

Place	Date	Hour	Summary of Events and Information	Remarks and references to Appendices
Sheet 27 V.17 c.76	16/8/18		Operation Order N° 11. Contd. VI Tools. Brigade reserve of tools will be carried when required, suitable arrangements.	
			VII Ammunition.	
			(a) 120 rounds per man and 2,000 per L.G. will be taken forward.	
			(b) Dumps. Dumps are established as under:-	
			U.18.d.4.3. – V.10.c.8.2. – V.15.a.5.1.	
			V.5.c.7.4. – U.24.a.3.5.	
			(c) Brigade dump (S.A.A. & 3" T.M.C.) at V.4.c.9.3.	
			(a) These dumps will be replenished at discretion of O.C. Units.	
			(c) Bde. H.Q. will be responsible for keeping its line transport filled with ammunition by S.A.A. Section at D.A.C.	
			VIII Medical.	
			(a) A.D.S. U.20.b.9.4. and V.1.a.9.5.	
			(b) Corps Walking wounded collecting station T.23.a.3.9.	

WAR DIARY
or
INTELLIGENCE SUMMARY.
(Erase heading not required.)

Army Form C. 2118.

Place	Date	Hour	Summary of Events and Information	Remarks and references to Appendices
Sheet 27 U.11.a.78	16/8/18		Operation Order No.11 (copy) at Appx. Stragglers posts.	
			(a) These are being established at :-	
			Sheet 36/ C.13.c.73. C.13.a.77. C.1.6.3.2.	
			" 27 y.26.6.82. Y.32.c.6.9. U.6.6.6.0. U.16.a.7.9.	
			U.6.d.04 P.32.a.92. P.27.d.24.	
			(b) On receipt of code word EVENOW following personnel will be sent to report to special Bde HQ, for work under APM	
			40th Division 1 NCO + 7 OR. The party to be detailed by O.C. L Coy.	
			Tactical Battalion in attack	
17/8/18			Carried on Battalion training - Brigade Sports	
18/8/18			Carried on Battalion training	
19/8/18			Carried on Battalion training	
20/8/18			Tactical exercise carried out by Brigade jointly commanded by Lt Col J.F. PLUNKETT DSO. MC DCM).	

WAR DIARY or INTELLIGENCE SUMMARY

Army Form C. 2118.

(Erase heading not required.)

Place	Date	Hour	Summary of Events and Information	Remarks and references to Appendices
Sheet 27 U.17.c.7.8	21/8/18		119th Inf. Bde. Operation Order No 19 received	
			Battalion moved to LE TIR ANGLAIS	
LE TIR ANGLAIS	22/8/18		119th Inf. Bde. Operation Order No 20 received	
			Battalion moved to front line and has overtaken at VIEUX BERQUIN	
			Line advanced 500 yards. Relief was completed without any casualty of note	
	23/8/18		Nothing of note.	
	24/8/18		119th Inf. Bde. Operation Order No 21 received	
			Heavy shelling of VIEUX BERQUIN by enemy artillery. 11 O.R. wounded.	
Sheet 36A NE E 23 b	25/8/18		Operation order No 13 issued. Ref sheet 36A NE 1/20,000.	
			1. An inter-company relief will take place tonight 25/26 Aug as follows:-	
			Front line. .... O'Coy will be relieved by b Coy	
			.... H .... - I	
			Support line. On relief G.H. Coys will move into Fouracres now occupied by J.I. Coys respectively.	

WAR DIARY
INTELLIGENCE SUMMARY

Army Form C. 2118.

Place	Date	Hour	Summary of Events and Information	Remarks and references to Appendices
Sheet 36a				
E.23.b	25/8/18		1) I & J Coys will not move from their present positions till 9 p.m.	
			2) Coys from G Coy for J Coy will be at Bn H.Q. at 8.30 p.m.	
			3) Guides from H Coy for I Coy will be at T.C. at HQ and Guides from Coy will be on platoon scale at 9 p.m.	
			4) S.A.A. & Grenades and any other trench stores to be handed out in particulars, receipt, one copy of which will be handed to Adjt by 9 a.m. 26/8/18	
			5) Completion of relief to be notified by the Coys with BATTn	
			6) Acknowledge	
	26/6/18		Nothing of note.	
			Operation Order No 14 issued - (copy attached)	
	27/8/18		Battalion advanced under cover of "creeping" barrage. Report attached. Casualties - 2/Lieut. A.S.SUMMERHAYES, 2/Lieut A.C.WILSON - Killed	

(a/CAPT)

WAR DIARY
or
INTELLIGENCE SUMMARY.
(Erase heading not required.)

Place	Date	Hour	Summary of Events and Information	Remarks and references to Appendices
Sheet 36a N.F.				
E.23.6	27/8/18		Wounded:- Capt. N.R.PROXBURGH. Capt. F.G.WHITE. Capt. W.F.MOSS. Lieut. G.H.JACKSON. 2/Lieut. F.M.COOPER. 2/Lieut. F.J.KILROE (Since died) 2/Lieut. E.A.CHAMPNEY. 2/Lieut. W.ROUTLEDGE. 2/Lieut. S.H.PARR. 21 OR killed, 141 OR wounded, 3 OR missing (believed killed). Battalion moved to "Z" Line with Batt. H.Q. at SWARTENBROUCH FARM (E.14.c.53)	
	28/8/18		119th Inf. Bde. Operation Order No 24 received. Operation order No 16 issued - (copy attached)	
	29/8/18		Battalion moved to Camp in D.21.a	
D.21.a	30/8/18		119th Inf. Bde Operation Order No 25 received.	
	31/8/18		General cleaning up and re-organising. Following officers reported for duty. Lieut. S.D.H.HARRISON. 2/Lt. J.A.PATTERSON. 2/Lt. F.W.SHARPE. 2/Lt. J.P.GRAY. 2/Lt. M.LARKMAN. 2/Lt. J.FINNEY M.C.	

3/9/18

SECRET.   13th Batt'n Inniskilling Fus'rs.
                                              Operation Order No. 14
Ref: Sheet 28.   14th June 1917.

The Batt'y with two platoons of the 12th Bn
North Staffordshire Reg't attached will carry out the
following operation tomorrow.

1. Objective. To take and consolidate the line
F.26.d.6.9 – L.3.c.7.9 – L.3.c.7.5 – L.8c.6.8.

Information. It is not expected that the enemy
will be encountered in force but machine guns
and snipers will probably form the opposition.

2. Method of Attack.
                    H. Coy on the left and G. Coy on the
right will form a wave with 25 yards between lines
and advance on either side of Peckets Corner –
Bishops Corner Road 350 yds to its east and 250 yds to
its west, road to be inclusive of H. Coy.
                    On reaching Bishops Corner H. Coy
will consolidate line L.3.a.6.4 – L.3.c.7.9 – L.3.c.4.6
and G. Coy pivotting its left on the right of H. Coy.
will swing round its right, take Rue Provost and
consolidate line from right of H. Coy to L.8.b.5.4.
I Coy moves from 50 yds in rear of H. Coy
and establishes a line of posts from F.26.d.9.9
to L.3.a.6.4 gaining touch with H. Coys left
post and with right post of 12th Bn North Staffs Reg't
which are side-stepping to the right and
forming a liaison post with the Batt'n at F.26.d.9.9
L Coy moves out 50 yds in rear of G. Coy and
travelling due south mops up all ground from
right of G. Coy to LAUDIER. Keeping touch with
the right of G. Coy it will consolidate on the line
L.8.b.5.4 – L.8.a.9.9.10.   When the right
standing barrage ceases at Zero + 72 the right
platoon assisted if necessary by a reserve
platoon of the North Staffs will take and
consolidate Bowery Cottages. The two platoons
of North Staffs will move 50 yds in rear of L. Coy.
            All lines except I Coy will move in a wave
with 25 yds between lines, men extended to about
5 paces. A mopping party of 1 N.C.O. and 6 men
to move about 30 yds in rear of the centre of
each Coy. I Coy will move forward in files
of sections.   Coys will be in position 50 yds

north of the road Rooster Farm - Beckets to F.26.b.67.7 at 3 A.M tomorrow and will rest until Zero - 30. Patrols returning at dawn.

3. About Zero + 120 the 120th Infy Bde will take over line Bishops Corner - Bowery Cottages. S Coy will then move to line about L.2.b Centre as right support and T Coy to about F.26.d.2.3 both facing east.

The two platoons of 12th Bn North Staffs. will rejoin their own unit.

The Battn remains on line F.26.d.9.9 - Bishops Corner inclusive.

4. The following is the Artillery programme for the attack.

(a) A creeping barrage of 54 - 18 pndrs will stand from Gillie Farm to the Lauzick. The barrage will be thickest on the left. Where It will come down at Zero in a line 300 yds in advance of Rooster Farm - Becket Corner Road and will move forward at Zero + 6 mins at the approx. rate of 100 yds in 3 minutes to a line Bowery Cottages - Hur Pivot - Prince Farm where it will remain as a protective barrage till Zero + 75 when it creeps forward again to a line about 300 yds south of the above road. At Zero + 90 this protective barrage will begin to roll up from West to East As the guns lift off they will switch on to a line Prince Farm - Regale Farm.

(b) In addition to the creeping barrage there will be a standing barrage mixed with smoke on the Lauzick from L.1.b.65.35 to L.14.d.77. This barrage will lift from L.2.0.21 at Zero + 60 and will cease altogether at Zero + 75.

(c) The ercaly Artillery will put down a standing barrage mixed with smoke on the line Gillie Farm - Prince Farm searching 400 yds eastwards to protect the left flank of the attack. This barrage will cease at Zero + 110.

(d) A heavy artillery standing barrage will be put down on the line of the road Bishops Corner to L.2.c.15.15.

At Zero + 21 lifts on to the Line Bowery
Cottages - Rue Provost - L.9.a.8.8 - Acton Cross
This Barrage will roll off at following times:-
   Zero + 65   off Bowery Cottages
     " + 90   .   Rue Provost
     " + 100   .   L.9.a.8.8
     " + 106   .   Regal Lodge
     " + 130   .   Yalton Farm & Acton Cross.

5 Infantry moves forward at Zero.

H Manning Capt & Adjt
13th Bn R. Innis. Fus.rs.

Notes.

(a) In addition to S.A.A. every second man in G, H & J. coys will carry two (2) hand grenades in bottom jackets pockets

(b) L.M.B's and M.G's attached will be allotted on objectives being taken

(c) Every endeavour must be made to keep within 25 yds of creeping barrage

(d) Forward communications from Bn Battle Hdqtrs will be arranged by the Bn Signalling Officer

(e) Prisoners will be brought to Bn Battle H.Qrs

(f) Watches will be synchronised at Bn Battle H.Q. at 8 a.m. tomorrow.

(g) Zero hour will be notified later.

(h) A contact aeroplane will fly over at Zero + 2 hours Ground Flares and discs will be shown.

2nd Bn. Roy Inn Killing Fus.

Confidential
Map Ref - Sheet 36ᵃ N.E.   28th Aug. 1918

Report on attack by above Batt. on 27th Aug 1918.

Task objective was to capture and consolidate line F.26.d.9.0. - L.3.c.6.9 - L.3.c.4.8. and capture Bowery Cottage, L.8.c.

(b) To mop up all ground between Becket Corner - Bishops Corner Road and Landeck, and Bishops Corner - Denver Road to Landeck, inclusive.

3/5 - At 10 a.m. the Artillery opened on programme and the Battn. advanced.

At 10.10 a.m. the line extended from about 300ˣ E. of Becket Corner - Bishops Corner Road, from right standing barrage which was practically along Landeck.

Enemy Artillery, Machine Guns, and Rifle fire had opened about 10.10 a.m. as the Artillery was on a line from N. to S. about 100ˣ E. of Landeck. It appears that he believed our attack to be to the E. instead of South. We suffered little from his Artillery.

From about 200ˣ N. of Bishops Corner Machine Gun Posts were encountered practically all along the line and our casualties were increasing rapidly. First one part of the line and then another was held up, but by individual initiative or orders, those on flanks of posts dealt with the gun commands and the advance continued, only parts of the line temporarily losing the creeping barrage. About on a line from E. to W. and 300ˣ N. of Bishops Corner Rifle Posts were encountered and overcome by the bayonet. The enemy put up a good fight at L.2.b.3.4. After the battle at this spot were counted 18 enemy bodies and 12 of ours. Similar encounters had taken place on the Becket Corner - Bishops Corner Road. Bishops Corner was held as a strongpoint

2

to the enemy, and when we were held up, Lce Cpl
Smiles, who by now had taken command of his
Coy (that with the commander and 2 other Officers of the
Coy being casualties) took up a frontal line and
[unclear] parties on either flank, the enemy line,
pushed the enemy from 3 sides. He enemy fled, but
left a Machine Gun and 4 wounded men in our
hands. Fire was opened on the retreating enemy.
Bishops Corner was now in our hands, time 12.50 am.
The Bishops Corner - Denver Road was also crossed
at this time along the whole of our front. A line of
posts was established from F.26.d.9.9 - L.3.a.6.4 - L.3.c.7.9,
L.3.c.4.8. The 2 Coy Commanders had become casualties
L. Coy on the right of the Bishops Corner, looking on its
left moved forward in centre and right, so as to pro-
long the line to about L.2.d.3.3. and F. Coy on the right
conformed Northwards. F. Coy moved on [unclear] under
Lt Hopes to attack Bowery Cottages. Lt Hales had
not proceeded far when Lt Hopes was hit near the
elbow, but remained with Pce [illegible]. The party were
about 300 x from Bowery Cottages when about 5
Machine Guns opened heavy fire on them and Lt
Hopes was again hit in the leg. I had warned
my Officers that the 120th Bde would advance at
2.30 + 90. He Hopes therefore decided to hold
on where he was until they came up. As the
120th Bde did not come forward I decided to
shorten my line on the right which was very thinly
held, and Lt Hopes's party withdrew to those
on right covering, my line with a defensive flank
ran F.26.d.9.9 - L.3.c.7.9 - L.3.a.8.0 - L.3.d.7.9. Sups
were sent up to me from Brigade. He hostile [fire]
from Bowery Cottages and [unclear] [illegible] swept
our front while right flank was [unclear]

3.

3. Our casualties in actual attack were 3 Officers Killed and 9 wounded, 15 Other Ranks killed and 60 wounded.

The enemy losses were about 50 killed, 28 prisoners taken, 2 Heavy and 6 Light Machine Guns and 3 Trench Guns (filled with leather cannisters) were taken by us.

Recommendations for acts of gallantry will be forwarded as soon as possible.

Hunter R. Holoroush

Lt.Col. 13/Roy. Innis. Fusrs.

27/8/18.

119/40

Confidential

War Diary
of
13th Bn. Royal Inniskilling Fusiliers

From 1/9/1918 To 30/9/1918

(VOLUME 1)

Army Form C. 2118.

WAR DIARY
or
INTELLIGENCE SUMMARY.
(Erase heading not required.)

Instructions regarding War Diaries and Intelligence Summaries are contained in F. S. Regs., Part II. and the Staff Manual respectively. Title pages will be prepared in manuscript.

Place	Date	Hour	Summary of Events and Information	Remarks and references to Appendices
Sheet 36a D.21.a	1/9/18		Battalion training. 119th Infantry Bde O.O. N°26 received. O.O. N°17 issued (copy attached)	
	2/9/18	1pm	Battalion moved to VIEUX BERQUIN area by march route	
		4pm	Arrived VIEUX BERQUIN - Tents & Shelters in camp.	
VIEUX BERQUIN	3/9/18		119th Infantry Brigade O.O. received	
	4/9/18		Battalion moved to LE CHIEN BLANC (A.2.d.)	
LE CHIEN BLANC	5/9/18	5.30pm	Battalion arrived. Tents & Shelters in camp.	
	6/9/18		119th Infantry Brigade Warning Order received - N°28. 119th Infantry Brigade O.O. N°29 received. Operation order N°18 issued. The Battalion took over line JESUS FARM (B.26.d 4.0.) to junction with 62nd Infantry Bde on right - from 2nd LANCASHIRE FUSILIERS.	
LETT FARM. B.25.c.3.6.	7/9/18		In line. Situation normal - 30 Other ranks wounded. 119th Infantry Brigade letter 91/27/G.L. received.	
	8/9/18		119th Infantry Brigade O.O. N°31 received. Capt. McLEOD wounded at duty. 2 other ranks wounded.	

WAR DIARY
or
INTELLIGENCE SUMMARY.
(Erase heading not required.)

Army Form C. 2118.

Place	Date	Hour	Summary of Events and Information	Remarks and references to Appendices
LETT FARM	8/9/18		Battalion relieved in outpost line by 13th E. LANCS REGT. - To reserve	
	9/9/18		Situation normal. 2 other ranks - wounded	
	10/9/18		Situation normal. 1 other rank - wounded	
POSTON FARM B.4.C.3.4.	11/9/18		Moved to support	
			1 OR WATERLANDS. 1 OR TIGER FARM	
			1 OR PUNGENT FARM. 1 OR TANDY FARM	
	12/9/18		193rd Infantry Brigade letter 93/28/6 received	
	13/9/18		"A" Support Line. Draft of 100 other ranks reported for duty	
			193rd Infantry Brigade O.O. No 33 received (copy attached)	
			O.O. No 19 issued Support by 15th KOYLI	
			Battalion relieved in Support by 15th KOYLI	
	13/9/18		Battalion arrived in Cauroy support area. En's billets	
LE CHIEN BLANC A.21.a.4.5.	14/9/18		Parties on training	
	15/9/18		Parties on training	
	16/9/18		Parties on training	
	17/9/18		Parties on training. Capt L.C. BADHAM and 1 O.R. attached for duty (copy attached)	
	18/9/18		Operation order No 20 issued	
	19/9/18		Parties on training	
	20/9/18		119th Infantry Brigade O.O. received	
			O.O. No 21 issued (copy attached)	
	21/9/18		Battalion moved by march route to BAILLEUL and thence by rail to HAZEBROUCK	
HAZEBROUCK			Lt Colls	

WAR DIARY
or
INTELLIGENCE SUMMARY.

(Erase heading not required.)

Army Form C. 2118.

Place	Date	Hour	Summary of Events and Information	Remarks and references to Appendices
HAZEBROUCK	22/9/18		Battalion cleaning up generally. Ten (10) officers reconnoitering new sector of line. 119th Infantry Brigade O.O. received.	
	23/9/18	7.45am	O.O. No.22 issued (copy attached). Battalion moved by rail to BAILLEUL.	
		11.30am	Battalion returned to HAZEBROUCK.	
	24/9/18		Re-organising Battalion.	
	25/9/18		Inspected by G.O.C. 119th Infantry Bde. 119th Infantry Brigade O.O. received. O.O. No.23 issued (copy attached)	
Sheet 36 N.W. B.10. & 25.20	26/9/18		Battalion moved by rail to BAILLEUL - thence by march route to line. Outpost line taken over. Pos. H.Q. B.10. & 25.20. (Sheet 36 N.W.)	
	27/9/18		5 prisoners taken. 2/Lieut. M. LARKMAN wounded. 1 other rank killed. 3 other ranks wounded. Outpost line taken over by 13th East Lancashire Regt. Battalion moved to support in NIEPPE SYSTEM	
	28/9/18		Reconstructing trenches in NIEPPE SYSTEM. 5 other ranks wounded.	
	29/9/18		2 posts established in NIEPPE SYSTEM - 4 other ranks wounded. 119th Infantry Brigade O.O. received. 2 other ranks wounded.	
	30/9/18		Operation order No.24 issued (copy attached)	

Army Form C. 2118.

WAR DIARY
or
INTELLIGENCE SUMMARY.
(Erase heading not required.)

Instructions regarding War Diaries and Intelligence Summaries are contained in F. S. Regs., Part II. and the Staff Manual respectively. Title pages will be prepared in manuscript.

Place	Date	Hour	Summary of Events and Information	Remarks and references to Appendices
B.12.Z.4.4.	30/9/8		Battalion took over outpost line from 13th EAST LANCASHIRE REGT. Line advanced. Following up retiring Bulgarians.	

[signature]
[signature]
Comdg. 13th R Sussex Regt.

B.Bn. Roy. Irish Rgs.
OPERATION ORDER No. 16.   Copy 8

1. Ref. sheet 36ᵃ/N.E. (edit. 7th trans.) + sheet 36ᵃ.
   MOVE. The Battn. will move tomorrow to camp in
   D 21. a. vacated by 23rd Bn. Cheshire Regt.

2. The Battn. will move off at 8.0 a.m. from present line in
   the following order. Battn. H.Q. B, A, D, C Coys.

3. Route from SWARTENBROUCK Farm, E. 19 b. 8. 8. – E. 13. c. 3.5. – E. 3. a. 0. 3.
   D. 11. d. 7. 6. – D. 16. d. 2. 3. – D. 21. d. 7. 6. – D. 21 a. 0. 2. The usual distance
   will be maintained between Coys. & Platoons.

4. Transport Officer will have L.S. limbers at each Coy H.Q. at 7.15 a.m.
   Officers kits & R. Blankets (which will be tied in bundles of ten
   with cord) will be dumped at Bn. & Coy H.Q. at 7.0 a.m.
   Transport Officer will have L.S. wagon to collect blankets &
   Officers kits from Bn. Coy. H.Q. at 7.0 a.m. A Guard will
   be left at each H.Q. until everything has been collected. The
   Guards will then join their Coys.

5. Riders for C.O. 2nd in Command, Adjutant & Coy Commdrs. will be
   at Bn. H.Q. at 7.45 a.m.

6. Mess Cart will be at Bn H.Q. at 7.30 a.m. Officers Mess Kits
   will be at Bn. H.Q. at 7.0 a.m. Masters Cart at Bn H.Q. 7.30 a.m.

7. 2 Limbers will be at Bn. H.Q. at 7.30 a.m. 1 for Signals
   & Medical Room & 1 for Canteen.

8. Qu. Stores & all Transport will move independently
   to Transport lines in. C. 6. b. 3.5.

9. Acknowledge.

Copy No 1   C.O.
        2   2 i/c
        3   A Coy
        4   B Coy
        5   C Coy
        6   D Coy
        7   Transport Officer
        8   War Diary
        9   File

H.H. Venning Capt. & Adjt.
B. Bn. R. Irish Rgs.

In the Field,
Aug 27. 1918.

SECRET.   13th Bn. K.R.R. Copy No.
                   OPERATION ORDER NO. 17

Ref. Map. 28 B.N.E. 1/10000

1. The Battn. will march to day 2/9/16 into BIVOUAC area.
   Headquarters details will move at 12 p.m. followed by H.H.I.G.J.
   300' distance between platoons.

2. Dress. Fighting Order.

3. Route. LENS ROAD — TARA REDAN — SPEARMINT CORNER — STENOGRAPHERS —
   E. 19 b. 8. 8. — GREEN FARM — NJERR BIVOUACS.

4. Packs, Blankets & Officers Kits will be dumped at present
   Q.M. Stores by 12 noon. Guard of 1 N.C.O. & 3 men over them to be
   detailed by R.S.M.

5. Riders for C.O. 2nd in Comd. Adjutant, Coy Comdrs Ch. O. will
   be at Bn H.Q. at 12.45 p.m. Their own feeders will report to O/C
   Coys at 12 noon.

6. Transport lines will be near ELA FARM in Square E22.a.
   Separate instructions have been issued to Transport Officer
   & Quartermaster.

7. Acknowledge.

                              F.H. Denning Captain & Adjt
                                             13th Bn K.R.R. Corps.
2/9/16.

Copy No. 1. C.O.
   ..   2. 2nd in Comd.
   ..   3. O/C G Coy
   ..   4.   H Coy
   ..   5.   I Coy
   ..   6.   J Coy
   ..   7. Transport Officer
   ..   8. Quartermaster
   ..   10. War Diary
   ..   11. File.

SECRET.   Copy No: 12

13th Bn Royal Inniskilling Fus.

Operation Order No. 18.

Ref maps. S.W.
  Sheet. 36A. N.E. 7b.
       " 36 N.W. 9a.

1. The 119th Infy Bde will relieve the 121st Infty Bde in the Advanced Guard of the 40th Divn. on 6th inst.

2. This Battn. will take over the front from Jeans Farm (B.26.d.4.0.) inclusive to junction with 182nd Infty Bde on the right.
"H" Coy 13th R. In is Fus will relieve "A" Coy 23rd Lancs Fus. taking over the right front from Essex post (inclusive) to Lancashire post (exclusive) and getting into touch with the 182nd Infty Bde on the right.
"J" Coy 13th R. Inis Fus will relieve "C" Coy 23rd Bn. Lancs Fus taking over the left front from Lancashire post (inclusive) to Jeans Farm (inclusive) and getting into touch with 13th East Lancs on left.
"G" Coy will take up a position in the vicinity of Lett Farm (B.26.c.3.0)
"T"   "   "   "   "   "   "   "   "   "   Waterlands (B.27.a.4.3.)

3. Guides will be at H.Q. 23rd Lancs Fus. (A.24.d.5.3) at 8.0 p.m. for "H" & "J" Coys. & will lead them to Essex Post & Lancashire Post respectively.

4. H.Q. Details will move at 8.0 p.m. followed by "T" & "G" Coys.

5. Bn H.Q. at Lett Farm. Location of R.A.P. to be notified later.
   S.a.a. Dump at Goshold Farm. A.30.c.30.75.

6. Completion of relief to be notified to Bde. H.Q. by Code Word "VENUS".

7. Separate instructions have been issued to Transport Officer & Quartermaster.

8. Acknowledge.

                                         W Kenning Capt & Adjutant
                                              13th Bn. R. In is Fus.

Copy No. 1. CO
   "   " 2. 2nd / comd.
   "   " 3. O/c. "G" Coy
   "   " 4. O/c. "H" Coy
   "   " 5. O/c. "T" Coy
   "   " 6. O/c. "J" Coy
   "   " 7. Quartermaster
              Transport Officer
   "   " 8. 23rd Lancs Fus.
   "   " 9. 119th Inf Bde.
   "   " 10. War Diary.
   "   " 11. File.
   "   " 12. Office.

18th in Divisional Res...
OPERATION ORDER No. 13.A.B.   Copy No. 1

Ref Map Sheet 36 N.W. 1/20,000   SECRET.

13/4/0

1. The 119 Inf. Brig. will be relieved by the 120 Inf. Brig. as advanced Guard to 40 Division on the night of Sept 13/14.

2. This Bn will be relieved in support by 15th K.O.Y.L.I. as follows:-
   D. Coy 15th K.O.Y.L.I. will relieve H Coy 13th E. Sur. Regt on the left
   C.   "   "   "   "   J "   "   "   in the centre.
   A.   "   "   "   "   I "   "   "   on the right
   B.   "   "   "   "   G "   "   "   in reserve

3. Guides on the scale of 1 Officer per Coy and one man per platoon will meet relieving Coys at cross Roads in B.19.a.2.1 at 7.45 p.m.

4. Trench stores will be handed over on relief, receipts being taken in duplicate. One Copy will be handed to Adjt by 9. a.m on 14th inst. All water & food containers which have been sent from Q.M. Stores will be taken. R.S.M. will hand over any stores at Bn. H.Q.

5. 1 Lewis Gun Limber per Coy will be at undermentioned locations for conveyance of L.Gs etc. at 9. p.m.
   H Coy at NIEPPE   16.b.5.3.
   I "   " ORVILLE JUNCTION
   J "   " TAFFY FARM.
   G "   " B.19. c. 7.7.

   In addition 2 Limbers will be at Bn H.Q. POSTON FARM at 8 p.m. for transport of Officers' Mess, Orderly Room, and Signalling Plat. Any further transport required for Cooks Gear etc. will be arranged between Q.M. & T.O.

6. Completion of relief to be notified to Bn H.Q. by word "CRUMPET"

7. On completion of relief Coys will proceed independently to F.21. d. 4.5 to camp now occupied by 15th K.O.Y.L.I.

8. The Q.Master will arrange for a hot meal to be served to the men on arrival and for Officers' Valises and men's packs being transported to new camp.

9. ACKNOWLEDGE.

Copy. No: 1. O.C
         2. B. Coy
         3. A "
         4. I "
         5. J "
         6. 12th North Staffs.
         7. 15th K.O.Y.L.I.
         8. T.O - Q.M.
         9. Adjt.
        10. R.S.M.
        11. War Diary
        12. Office

D.V. Heming Capt. & Adjt.
13th Bn E. Surrey Regt

13th Bn Royal Inniskilling Fusiliers

SECRET.   Operation Order No. 20   Copy No.

Ref Sheet (Morris) 36ᵃ N.W. 1/20000   18/9/16
           36 N.W. 1/20000

Instructions for Defence of Divisional Battle Line

Divisional Battle Line
(i) The Divl. Battle line will be the line of the STEENBECQUE RIVER. This line represents the front of the position on which the Division will stand & fight in the event of a heavy hostile counter attack.

(ii) The 119th Infty Bde. is responsible for the defence of this line
    (a) The right subsection will be held by the 13th Bn Royal Innis Fus, the left by the 12th N Staffs Regt.
    The 13th E Lancs Regt will be in Divisional Reserve.
    (b) C & D Coys. 39th MG Corps are allocated to the Brigade for the defence of this line.

(iii) Other Units in Divisional Reserve
    (a) Reserve Infty Bde at present in the Hazebrouck Area.
    (b) 12th Bn Worcestershire Regt (P) & Field Coys RE

2. **Principles to be adopted for the Defence of the Divl Battle Line**

(a) **Infantry**
    (i) There will be two lines of Defence, namely:- The Outpost line & the Line of Resistance.

(ii) **Outpost Line.** It will be the line of Observation & will be held by one (1) Platoon of G, I, & J Coys.
    The object of this line is to give warning of the approach of the enemy troops holding the Line of Resistance.

Disposition

J Coy Coy HQ	at	G 11 a 1 6
Sentry Groups No. 1		G 11 a 3 5
No. 2		G 11 a 35 35
No. 3		G 5 c 45 05
I Coy Coy HQ	at	G 5 c 05 95
Sentry Groups No. 4		G 5 a 3 4
No. 5		G 5 c 35 95
No. 6		G 5 a 4 5
G Coy Coy HQ	at	A 29 c 3 7
Sentry Groups No. 7		A 29 c 45 15
No. 8		A 29 c 80 45
No. 9		A 29 a 80 15

(iii) **Line of Resistance**
    The Line of Resistance will be held by G, I, & J Coys. finding their own outposts (G on the left, I in the centre & J on the right.)

Disposition
J Coy - 1 Platoon on Steenwerck Switch with its left covering the road at A 29 a 2 3.
1 Platoon on Steenwerck Switch with its right crossing the road at G 11 b 7 8
Coy HQ & 1 Platoon in reserve at A 23 d 4 9

-(Contd)-

2

I Coy — 1 Platoon on Stonewerk trench will have its left
communication trench G.4.b.3.
1 Platoon on Stonewerk trench with its rt
at G.4.d.7.7.
Coy HQ and 1 Platoon in reserve trench at G.4.d.3.3.

J Coy — 1 Platoon on Stonewerk trench with its right at
house at G.4.d.6.0.
1 Platoon with it centre on main Railway at
G.10.b.33
Coy HQ and 1 Platoon in reserve at G.10.b.1.8

Bn HQrs at G.4.a.35.15 (La Petit Mortier)

R A P

H Coy in reserve at Bde HQrs

(III) Dividing Line Between Coys —
        I Coy Southern G.5.c.7.4 – G.4.d.2.4 inclusive
        I " Northern G.5.a.6.8 – G.4.b.1.9 inclusive

3/ ACTION IN CASE OF HOSTILE COUNTER ATTACK
(1) The Bn will be prepared to man the Downside of
Bocelle line one hour after receipt of order from Bde
HQrs to "Stand to"
(2) On receipt of the order "Stand to"
(a) The Batn less Transport will fall in on its
alarm Post at A.21.d.0.6. (La Croix Blanche) and await orders
(b) 1st line Transport
(i) All horses will be harnessed but not "hooked in"
(ii) Teams for Transports at Bde. Bn Camp will depart
immediately at their respective Coy HQ
(iii) A mounted orderly from the Bn Transport will
report to Bde HQ

4 On Receipt of the order "Man Line" the Batt will
man its alarm sectors
1st line Transport
(1) All Transport at Camp other than farrier, lenders &
lenders detailed as Batt sector Res. S.A.A. will proceed
to Transport lines
(ii) Animals will be saddled and Transport will be ready
to move at shortest notice

5 Boundaries
(i) Divisional Southern P.8.9.10.11 Central
              Northern A.15.16.17.18 Central
(ii) Sub Sector A.29.a.6.5. A.28.b.9.5.60. A.28.b.0.5. along
track running N.W. to A.21.d.5.6

6 Ammunition Reserve
(a) Rifle Ammunition
18,000 Rounds S.A.A. to be kept on wheels with Teams
handy at present Bn HQ
(b) Brigade Reserve
36,000 Rounds S.A.A. on wheels at Bde HQ. One
lendered G.S. Wagon with 18,000 Rds S.A.A. to be
sent to Bde HQ by this Battn on receipt
of order "Man Line"

TRENCH MORTARS
On receipt of the order "Stand to" one L G.S. Wagon
of this Batt will report to Bde HQ for the purpose
of carrying T.M.C.

contd.

3

7. Companies will each have a complement of 2 S.O.S Grenades and a reserve of 4 will be at Bn HQ

2 Boxes 1" Very Lights and 1 Box Red Flares will be kept at Batt HQ for issue to Coys going into action

In addition to above the Battn will be prepared –

(a) To assemble in squares A 16 22 & 28
(b) To move forward to support the front line Brigade
(c) To counter-attack to retake the NIEPPE line

8. Acknowledge

James Mann
Lt
a/Adjt.
13th Bn R. Innis. Fus.

Copy No. 1 CO
2 2nd I/C
3 HQ 119 Bde
4 To G Coy
5   ” H
6   ” I
7   ”
8 Transport Officer
9 Quartermaster
10 War Diary
11 File
12 MGC

SECRET.   13th Bn. ROYAL INNISKILLING FUSILIERS
                                                    Copy No. 2
               OPERATION No 21.
Ref: Sheets 36 }
             27 } 1/20,000
             36 }

1. The 119th Infantry Bde will relieve the 151st Infty Bde in Reserve Bde area on 21st Sept. 1918.

2. This Bn will relieve the 23rd Cheshire Regt (H.Q. D.3.b.9.2.)

3. The Battn will move to Hazebrouck tomorrow by train from BAILLEUL Station. H.Q. & Coys will parade at 8-45 a.m. and will move off in the following order: H.Q., G, H, I, J Coys with 100x distance between Coys. H.Q. Coys will render a return to the Orderly Room by 4 p.m. tonight, shewing their entraining strength. Dress - Musketry Order - Steel Helmet, Haversack at side.

4. Each Coy will detail 1 Officer & NCO as an advance party. Officers detailed will report to the Adjutant at 9 p.m. tonight for instructions. This party will rendezvous at Bn HQ at 7-0 am to move off. Officers on horseback, NCOs on bicycle. The Signal Officer & N.C.O. from H.Q. will accompany this party. N.C.Os will get bicycles at Bn H.Q.

5. Blankets packs will be stacked by Coys at Bn H.Q. by 8-30 am. Blankets will be tightly rolled in bundles of 10 and labelled. Packs will have an identifying mark on them. Packs will have supporting straps arranged so that men can put them on at once.

6. Officers Valises, Officers Mess Kits will be dumped at Bn HQ by 7-30 am. Lewis Gun Limbers & Maltese Cart will be packed ready to move at 7-45.

7. Loading party to load lorries with blankets packs at Bn H.Q. will be detailed by R.S.M. J Coy will detail a loading party of 1 Officer & 40 other ranks to load Bn Stores and blankets on train at Bailleul Station. On arrival of lorries at station, this party will at once stack packs by Coys and Coys will file past their stack, each man taking a pack. This party will move off at 7-30 a.m. & will be at Bailleul Station by 9-15 a.m. The Officer i/c party will report to Adjutant at 9-45 am for instructions.

8. Coys will detail a N.C.O. to take charge of each wagon or compartment. After entrainment no man will be allowed to leave the train without the permission of an officer.

9. On arrival at Hazebrouck advance officers will meet Bn & guide H.Q. Coys to their Billets.

10. Separate instructions have been issued to Transport Officer.

11. Location of new Transport lines D.10.d.9.7.

12. All ammunition pack saddlery water tins (in excess of establishment) will be handed over & taken over respectively and receipts in duplicate exchanged. Receipts will be handed to Adjutant by 9-0 am 22 inst.

13. Acknowledge.

Copy No. 1 C.O.
        2   2nd i/c
        3   O/C G Coy
        4   "   H.   "
        5   "   I.   "
        6   "   J.
        7   T.O.
        8   Q.master
        9   R.S.M.
       10 War Diary.   No 11 Office.

                                    F.W. Fleming Capt. & Adjt.
                                    13th Bn. R. Inniskn Fus.

13 Bn. Royal Inniskilling Fusiliers

SECRET

Operation Order No 22

Ref map Sheet
36 N.W. & 28 S.W. 1/20,000

1. The 109th Inf Bde will take over part of the Sector at present held by the 9th Inf Bde on the night 23/24th Sept 1916.

2. The boundaries of the Bde Sector will be:-
   Southern Boundary B.7 cent - 16 cent & 18 cent.
   Northern   "   C.1.cent - B.5.c.35 - along road
                      b.3.10 & B.5.b.0 - B.5.b.o.o - A.16.a.6.4.

3. At the time of relief the Sector will be held by one Battn of the 9th Inf Bde. viz 12 Royal Scots. V.B. B.10.B.2.3.

4. The Bde Sector will be held by two Battns, this Battn on the right and 13th East Lancs Regt on the left, both with Bn H.Q. at B.10.b.23.
   Inter-Battn Boundary - Railway at B.12.b.0.5. Lancashire Junction (inclusive to left Battn) - B.11.a.0.0 (approx)

5. H Coy of this Battn will take over the right Sector of the Battn frontage.
   G Coy of this Battn will take over the left Sector of the Battn frontage.
   Inter-Coy Boundary - road running through B.11.d & 18.a. (inclusive to H Coy).
   I & F Coys will take up position in support with the NIEPPE System.
   F Coy between B.16.b.9.5. - B.11.c.0.4. (approx)
   G Coy   "   B.11.c.0.4. & B.10.b.9.4.
   Arrangements as to guides will be a later duty.

6. The Battn will unroot BAIZIEUX by rail tomorrow morning.
   H.Q. details & Coys will assemble at Bn H.Q at 4.15.a.m. ready to move off.
   Dress. Fighting Order, but haversack will be carried on the backs slung on supporting strap .... packs to be marked with letter of Coy.
   Officers kits, & Blankets (tightly packed in bundles of ??) will be at Coy H.Q by 4.15 a.m. Coys will detail loading parties.
   Officers mess Boxes not put in L.G Limbers are be at Bn H.Q by 4.15 a.m.
   L.G. Limbers will be loaded at Bn Stores at 4.45 a.m. Each Coy will send one NCO & pack to Limbers. The NCO will accompany the Limbers by Road.
   Officers trench kit may be put on L.G. Limbers.

Cont'd.

8. Baggage Party 1 officer & 30 o.r. [unclear] [unclear]
[unclear] [unclear]. This party will be at Boyen at [unclear]
[unclear] & will unload [unclear] officers [unclear] &
Lazy [unclear] & [unclear] at B [unclear]
9. They will load S.S. wago at [unclear] with notes
Packs, officers valises
10. Location of new transport lines will be
[unclear] of [unclear] Sand Pock (Ref. A 6.30.5.) field
near cross roads being avoided.
   Transport officer will act as adjutant in
[unclear] as possible of map Ref of [unclear] selected.
11. All ammunition [unclear] [unclear] [unclear] stores will be
taken over & receipts given taken. The receipts will be
handed to adjutant at 6.30 a.m. [unclear] aug 16. Map
Ref 5 Dumfos will be given.
12. Transport officer will detail a mounted orderly
to report to Bde H.Q. (B.2.C.V.) by 5.00 a.m. 22 aug &
maintain communication with transport lines.
These on duty will take 2 days rations with him
13. Completion of Relief to be notified to adjutant. Code
code word "BOOTS"
   Coys will notify the adjutant at once of
location of Coy H.Q. & will send a runner to Bn
H.Q. who knows the route to Coy H.Q.
14. Separate instructions have been issued to transport
officers
15. Reveille tomorrow will be 5.30 a.m. Breakfast
at 6.15 a.m.
16. Acknowledge

Copy No. 1. C.O.
   2 2 i/c
   3 Rt Ly Coy
   4 [unclear]
   5 [unclear]
   6 [unclear]
   7 M.O.
   8 [unclear]
   9 Q.M.
   10 R.S.M.
   11 [unclear]
   12 War diary

James Mann
S.P.
Capt
1 Bn. R. [unclear]
[unclear]

13th 7th East Yorks Regt. Transmission Sheet
Copy No. 11

SECRET   OPERATION ORDER No 23.

Ref Map Sheet
        36" N.W. 28.S.W. 1/20,000

1. The 119th Infty Bde will take over the right Batt sector at present held by the 92nd Inf Bde on the night 26/27 Sept. 1918.

2. The Boundaries of the Bde sector will be:-
        Southern Boundary   B.17 cent - 16 cent & 15 cent.
        Northern   "   C.1. cent - B.5.c.35 - along road
                    to B.10.a.8.5. 80 - B.9.b.1.4. - A.16.a.6.4.

3. At the time of relief the sector will be held by 10th Bn. East Yorks Regt.   H.Q. B.10.b.15.20.

4. The Bde sector will be held by 2 Battns, this Battn on the right and 13th E. Lancs Regt on the left, with this Battn H.Q. at B.10.b.25.20.
        Inter-Battn Boundary. Railway at B.12.b.3.5,
    Harrisburg Junction (incl. to left Battn) B.11.a.0.0. (approx)

5. H Coy of the Battn will take over the right sector of the Battn frontage.
    G Coy of the Battn will take over the left sector of the Battn frontage.
        Inter Compy Boundary - Road running through
    B.11.d & 18.a. (inclusive to H Coy)
        E & F Coys will take up positions in support in the NIEPPE system.
        E Coy between B.16.b.9.5 - B.11.c.0.4. (approx)
        F "   "   B.11.c.0.4 - B.10.b.9.4. (approx)
    Arrangements as to Guides will be notified later.

6. The Battn will move to BAILLEUL by rail tomorrow morning.
        H.Q. details & Coys will assemble at Bn H.Q. at 7.45 a.m. ready to move off.
    Dress - Fighting Order but Haversack will be carried on the packs slung on supporting straps (Men's packs must all be marked with letter of Coy.)

7. Officers Kits & Blankets (tightly rolled in bundles of Ten (10) will be at Coy H.Q. by 7.15 a.m. Coys will detail loading parties.
        Officers' Mess Boxes, not put on L.G. Limbers will be at Bn H.Q. by 7.45 a.m.
    L.G. Limbers will be loaded at Qr. Stores at 7.45 a.m. Each Coy will send one N.C.O. to pack the Limbers, this N.C.O will accompany the Limbers by Road.
    Officers Tech. Kit may be put on L.G. Limbers
                    contd.

2.

9. A Baggage Party of 1 officer & 30 O.Ranks will be detailed by "G" Coy. This party will be at Hazebrouck Station at 8.0 a.m., will load blankets & Officers' Valises at Hazebrouck and unload at Bailleul.

They will load G.S. Wagons at Bailleul with packs, blankets, Officers' Valises.

10. Location of new Transport lines will be near to road running through 36/A.4.a to 36/A.4.a.

Transport Officer will notify Adjutant as soon as possible of map reference of location selected.

11. All ammunition, area & trench stores will be taken over & receipts given & taken. These receipts will be handed to Adjutant at 6.30 a.m. 27-9-18. Map reference of dumps will be given.

12. Transport officer will detail a mounted orderly to report to Bde. H.Q. (B.8.a.4.2.) by 5.0 p.m. 26/9 to maintain communication with Transport Lines.

This orderly will take 3 days rations with him.

13. Completion of relief to be notified to Adjutant by Code Word "Boors".

Coys will notify to Adjutant at once of location of Coy H.Q. & will send a runner to Bn. H.Q. who knows the route to Coys H.Q.

14. Separate instructions have been issued to Transport Officer.

15. Reveille tomorrow will be 5.30 a.m. Breakfast at 6.15 a.m.

16. Acknowledge.

Copy No. 1. C.O.
 "   " 2. 2nd i/c
 "   " 3. "G" Coy
 "   " 4. "H" Coy
 "   " 5. "I" Coy
 "   " 6. "J" Coy
 "   " 7. Transport Officer
 "   " 8. Quartermaster
 "   " 9. R.S.M.
 "   " 10. War Diary. ✗
 "   " 11. File
 "   " 12. Office

G.H. Armour
Captain & Adjutant
13 Bn. R. Innis. Fus.

In the field. September 25/9/18

For operations on 27th August 1918 at
VIEUX BERQUIN.

2nd Bar to Distinguished Service Order

Capt (T/Lt. Col.) J.F. Plunkett. D.S.O. M.C. D.C.M.

Military Cross

Capt & Adjt.	D.P. Fleming	Scottish Rifles
Lieut	J.W. Petrie	Kings L'pool Regt.
T/2nd Lieut	F.M. Cooper	Northumberland Fus.
T/2nd Lieut	S. Smiles	Labour Corps

Military Medal

47293	a/C.S.M.	G. Findlay
47655	C.S.M.	P. Connor
47805	a/C.S.M.	R. Reeve
47796	a/Corpl.	H. Summersgill
48561	Corpl.	J. Gibbs
47560	a/L/Cpl.	W. Foundling
47486	a/L/Cpl.	E. Dupérey
47398	Pte.	R. Scott
48240	"	E. Walsh
48149	"	P. Gallacher
48226	"	W. McIntyre

For operations on 12th September 1918
at NIEPPE

Military Medal

47947 Pte. W. Parker.

SECRET.   13th R Innuskilling Fus.

Ref: Map sheet 36NW   Operation Order No. ___
     1/20000

1. The Bn. will take over the duties of Vanguard from 13th E. Lancs Regt. the night Sept 30/Oct 1.

2. The Coys of this Bn. will take up the positions which have already been pointed out to them. On these positions being occupied O.C. Coy will inform the O.C. Coy 13th E. Lancs Regt concerned who will then move off.

3. Completion of relief to be notified to Bn. H.Q. by code word ALLEZ. Bn. H.Q. B.6.c.55.20

4. R.A.P at B.12.a.9.8. Dump of S.A.A. etc will be established at ⓈB.12.b.3.4.

5. Trench Stores will be handed over and receipts handed to the Adjutant as soon as possible. 1 N.C.O + man per Coy will be left behind to look after Coy Stores as already instructed and this N.C.O will see that all food containers + water tins are returned to Bn. H.Q.

6. Acknowledge.

30/9/18   B. V. Heming Capt & Adj
                                     13th R Inniskilling Fus

War Diary

13th R. Inniskilling Fus

Month of October

Confidential

War Diary of the 13th Bn. Royal Inniskilling Fusiliers

From 1/10/18 To 31/10/18

(VOLUME I.)

WAR DIARY
or
INTELLIGENCE SUMMARY
(Erase heading not required.)

Army Form C. 2118.

Place	Date	Hour	Summary of Events and Information	Remarks and references to Appendices
Sheet 36NW. B.12.6.4.5	1/10/18		Patrols very active. Line further advanced. LE BIZET taken. 19th Infantry Brigade Wire. B.M.21 received. Casualties 1 O.R. wounded	
			B.M.98	
			B.M.100	
C.13.6.6.1	2/10/18		Line of Lys taken. Bridges being erected. Patrols in ARMENTIÈRES. 19th Infantry Bn wire B.M.1 received. Casualties: 1 O.R. killed	
			S.C.435	
			- 4 wounded	
			B.M.12	
Lys Post	3/10/18		Lys crossed at C.15.d.6.8. Bn H.Q. established at Lys Post. 3 Coys advanced through HOUPLINES SECTOR and occupied old BRITISH FRONT LINE. Slight opposition met. Casualties 4 O.R wounded. Telegram A.144 received. Operation order No 19 issued (copy atta)	
	3/4/10/18		Battalion relieved in front line by 12th N. Staffs Regt. Battalion moved to LE BIZET.	
LE BIZET	4/10/18		Battalion in huts in LE BIZET - Brigade Reserve. Casualties:- 4 OR wounded. Report on operations nights 1/2-2/3 of Oct. Bn (copy attached)	
	5/10/18		In Brigade Reserve. Casualties:- 1 O.R. wounded. 119th Infantry Brigade Operation order received. Battalion moved to NIEPPE SYSTEM.	

WAR DIARY or INTELLIGENCE SUMMARY.

Army Form C. 2118.

Place	Date	Hour	Summary of Events and Information	Remarks and references to Appendices
B.10.b.0.5	6/10/18		Carried on training and preparing NIEPPE SYSTEM.	Casualties:- 1 O.R wounded.
	7/10/18		Carried on training and repairing NIEPPE SYSTEM	
B.9.d.8.6	8/10/18		Carried on training and repairing NIEPPE SYSTEM	
	9/10/18		Carried on training and repairing NIEPPE SYSTEM.	
	10/10/18		Carried on training and repairing NIEPPE SYSTEM.	
	11/10/18		Scheme of Defence for NIEPPE SYSTEM issued (copy attached) 119th Infantry Brigade letter 6/3/9 received. Operation Order No.741 received.	
	12/10/18		Operation Order No 24 issued (copy attached) Battalion moved to LE CHIEN BLANC	
LE CHIEN BLANC	13/10/18		In billets and huts. Carried on with training	
	14/10/18		Carried on with training	
	15/10/18		Carried on with training	
	16/10/18		Carried on with training at 119th Infantry Brigade Operation Order No 42 received (copy attached) Operation Order No 25 issues (copy attached) Battalion moved to NIEPPE SYSTEM	
B.9.d.8.6.	17/10/18		119th Infantry Batt Telegram GT752 received. Operation Order N°43 received	

Army Form C. 2118.

WAR DIARY
or
INTELLIGENCE SUMMARY.
(Erase heading not required.)

Instructions regarding War Diaries and Intelligence Summaries are contained in F. S. Regs., Part I. and the Staff Manual respectively. Title pages will be prepared in manuscript.

Place	Date	Hours	Summary of Events and Information	Remarks and references to Appendices
B.9.a.8.6	17/10/18		Operation order No. 26 issued (copy attached)	
	18/10/18	03·00	Amendment to 119th Inf. Bde O.O. 43 received	
			Priority telegram from 119th Inf. Bde received	
SK N6 J.1.a.9.1			Battalion moved to outskirts of PERENCHIES - Huts	
	19/10/18		Working parties on railway, clearing away obstacles	
	20/10/18		Working parties on railway. Clearing away obstacles	
	21/10/18		Working parties on railway. Clearing away obstacles	
			Military medal ribbons presented to Sgt. ALEVI by Division Commander	
	22/10/18		Carried on Battalion training	
			119th Inf. Bde O.O. No 44 received	
	23/10/18		O.O. No 27 issued - copy attached	
	24/10/18		Battalion moved by march route to BONDUES	
BONDUES			Battalion arrived - billets	
	25/10/18		119th Infantry Brigade telegram G.T.858 received	
			Carried on Battalion training	
			119th Infantry Brigade O.O. No 45 received	
			Telegram G.T.871 received	
			" G.T.867 received	
			Operation order No 28 issued	

Army Form C. 2118.

WAR DIARY
or
INTELLIGENCE SUMMARY.
(Erase heading not required.)

Instructions regarding War Diaries and Intelligence Summaries are contained in F. S. Regs., Part II. and the Staff Manual respectively. Title pages will be prepared in manuscript.

Place	Date	Hour	Summary of Events and Information	Remarks and references to Appendices
BONDUES	26/10/18		Battalion moved to WATTRELOS	
	27/10/18		Carried on Battalion Training	
	28/10/18		Carried on Battalion Training	
	29/10/18		Carried on Battalion Training	
			Enemy mine exploded – following casualties	
			Officers:- Killed:- 2/Lt. J.C. NAPIER	
			Died of Wounds:- Capt. H.J. FREEMAN – 2/Lt. S.D.H. NARRISON	
			Wounded Major D.P. FLEMING	
			2/Lt. J. L. FOULDS	
			Other Ranks :- Killed 3	
			Missing Believed Killed. 1.	
			Wounded 6	
	30/10/18		Carried on Battalion Training	
	31/10/18		Carried on Battalion Training	
			119th Infantry Brigade O.O. 46 received	
			" Telegram G.T. 919 received	
			Operation Order No. 29 issued	

Comdg. 19th [Service?] Bn.

2.

Three unwounded and one wounded of the enemy surrendered.

Machine Gun and rifle fire of the enemy in front of my right flank during the night was fairly heavy.

The prisoners appeared to be very much surprised to find us holding our new line.

About 4 p.m. yesterday an enemy low flying aeroplane was forced to land in his own lines about I.5.d.

Our casualties during these operations were 2 other ranks killed. 22 other ranks wounded. No missing.

Hendrik
Lt. Colonel.
Comdg. 13th R. Innis. Fus.

4/10/18.

Headquarters,
119th Infantry Brigade.

With reference to my report on yesterday's operations, the position on the right was incorrect. The old British front line was taken from river LYS on left to C.29.a.0.1. on the right. The right company took the line C.28.a.0.1. to railway at I.3.d.0.2. The right company has an advanced platoon post at FORT EGAL at I.4.c.8.5.

The enemy attempted to raid one of my posts C.23.a.2.1. with a party estimated to be about 50 last night, but were beaten back by rifle and Lewis Gun fire, suffering casualties.

My post, consisting of 1 officer and 14 other ranks, at C.23.a.05.50. was also raided by a party of the enemy of about 20 or 30 last night, who approached and got within bombing distance. My post met the enemy with rifle and Lewis Gun fire. By this means, a portion of the enemy who tried to get round the left flank of post, was cut off by our fire, 5 of them surrendering this morning at SUSSEX AVENUE.

At 2 a.m. to-day my post at C.17.c.4.3. was attacked by a party of the enemy of about 20. The officer in charge of this post, who had 12 men under him, heard the enemy approaching and, holding his fire until the enemy was within 50 yards, then opened with Lewis Gun and rifle fire. After casualties had been inflicted on him the enemy retired. Later in the morning the officer heard a party of the enemy in front, apparently removing his wounded. Our post opened fire. It was now daylight, and the officer in charge of the post, seeing four of the enemy in a shell hole, advanced, accompanied by his Sergeant, and, throwing a bomb at them, called upon them to surrender.

13th Bn. Royal Inniskilling Fusiliers.

SECRET.   Scheme for Defence of NIEPPE SYSTEM.

Ref. Map. Sheet 36 N.W. 1/20000.

1. During the period that the Bde. is in support, it will be responsible for the upkeep and if necessary defence of the Nieppe System from the R.Lys at H.4.T.6.6 to N.Div. Boundary at B.4.d.4.2.

2. This Bn. will be responsible for the left Bn. sector the dividing line between Bn. sectors in the line being the grid line B.15.c.0.0 – B.17.c.0.0.

3. The defence of the Nieppe System will be organised on two lines viz. (1) the outpost line, (2) the main line of Resistance. The outpost line will be the trenches running through B.17.d. & c. to B.17 central and thereafter the line of the R. Warnave. The main line of Resistance will be the Nieppe System. Both these lines must be held to the last man and there must be no retreat from them.

4. The outpost line will be held by G. Coy with posts as follows :—
    B.17.c.95.40
    B.17.c.95.95
    B.17.b.4.3
    B.18.a.15.90
    B.12.c.4.2
    B.12.a.0.9
    B.12.b.70.35
    B.6.d.8.2

Coy. H.Qrs. Oosthove Farm.

5. The Nieppe System will be held by two Coys, I Coy on the right and J Coy on the left, the dividing line between Coys being the road at B.11.c.2.5 (incl. to J. Coy).

Posts will be established as follows :—

    I. Coy.   J. Coy.
    B.16.d.75.30   B.11.c.2.6
    B.16.b.90.70   B.11.c.10.80
    B.16.b.95.25   B.10.b.95.20
    B.16.b.95.50   B.10.b.85.50
    B.17.a.1.8   B.10.b.75.65
    B.11.c.15.15   B.10.b.60.90
    B.10.d.1.4   B.4.d.0.1
    Coy. H.Qrs. B.16.b.5.6   B.4.d.5.3
                                Coy. H.Qrs. B.10.b.70.25

6. H. Coy will be in support in closure in B.10.b.4.2.
   Bn. H.Q. at B.10.b.3.4.   R.A.P. at B.10.a.7.7.

7. On receipt of the order "Man the Nieppe System" Coys will at once man their respective positions and report to Bn. H.Q. on completion of move.

10/10/18.

(Sgd) D P Fleming Capt.
Commdg. 13th R. Innis. Fus.

SECRET.

13th Bn Royal Inniskilling Fusiliers.
OPERATION ORDER No. 28
10-10-18

Copy No. 2

Ref./Map - Sheet 36 N.W. 1/20,000
        36 S.E. 1/20,000

1. All indications point to the enemy preparing an early withdrawal in front of the 40th Division.

2. The objectives allotted to the Division are as follows:-
FORT DE LOMPRET (J.8.b) - Buildings (J.3.c.1.8) - LA TUILLERIE FARM (D.27.d.0.7) - LA CROIX TOURET, D.22.b.0.1 - QUESNOY (ensr)

3. The 119th Inf. Bde. will move to camps vacated by 120th Inf. Bde. in the NIEPPE - ERQUINGHEM Area on 17/10/18 and will remain in Divisional Reserve.

4. The Battalion will move to NIEPPE SYSTEM. H.Q at B.9.d.8.6. Coys will go to same positions in trench as they occupied before.

5. The Battalion will be ready to move off at 0845 hours in the following order:-
   Bn. H. Qrs. G. H. I. J. Coys.
   DRESS :- FIGHTING ORDER.

6. Advance parties of 1 Officer & 3 other ranks from each Coy and Bn. H.Q will move off at 0700 hours to prepare camp for arrival of Battalion.

7. Packs & blankets (tied in bundles of 10) will be dumped at Coy H. Qrs. by 0800 hours.

8. Officers' valises and Officers' Mess Kits will be at Q.M. Store by 0830 hours. Maltese cart at Bn. H.Q at 0830 hrs. Limber for Orderly Room & Signal gear at 0830 hours.

9. J. Coy will detail 1 NCO & 3 men as guard over present camp. They will be rationed by Q.M.

10. Transport Officer will make all necessary arrangements for transport of packs, blankets, valises etc to new camp.

11. Transport Lines at B.10.c.3.9.

12. ACKNOWLEDGE.

Copy No 1. C.O.
     " 2. O/C G. Coy
     " 3. " H
     " 4. " I
     " 5. " J
     " 6. Transport Officer
     " 7. Quartermaster.
     " 8. R.S.M.
     " 9. War Diary
     " 10. File
     " 11. Office

James Mann
2/Lt
a/Adjt
13th Bn Royal Innis. Fus.

119th Inf. Bde.

13th R. Innis. Fus.
13th E. Lancs Regt.
12th N. Staffs Regt.
119th T. M. B.
---

1. The Bde will relieve the 121st Inf. Bde in the Reserve Area (CHIEN BLANC - GD BEAUMART - N. of STEENWERCK) on Oct. 12th 1918.
    The 121st Inf. Bde relieves the Bde on the same day in the support area.

2. Details will be issued later.

Capt.
Bde. Major.
119th Inf. Bde.

11/10/18.

SECRET.   15th R. Innis Fus.   Copy No. 11.
                 Operation Order No 24

Ref- Map 36 N.W. (Edition 9a.)   11/10/18.
     1/20.000

1. The 119th Inf. Bde. will relieve the 121st Inf. Bde. in the
   Divisional Reserve Area and will be relieved in its support
   by 121st Inf. Bde. on 12/10/18.
2. The Battalion will be relieved in support by 23rd Bn
   Lancs. Fus.
3. On relief the Battn. will take over Camp at present occupied
   8th K. Irish Regt. Bn H.Q. A27.65.8. Transport will move to
   A28.6.1.9. Q.M. Stores A27.6.5.8. Dress: fighting order.
4. The Battn. will move off at 14.00 hours in the following
   order. Bn H.Q, G.H. I & J. Coys.
5. All defence schemes, photos, special maps, training
   facilities - also trench stores & ammunition will be
   handed over to 23rd Bn Lancs Fus. - and receipts given
   and taken. Receipts to be handed to Adjutant by
   09.00 hours 13/9/18.
6. Officers' Valises & Mess Kits and men's Packs will be
   stacked at Coy H.Q by 13.30 hours and a Guard of
   1 N.C.O. & 1 Pte placed over them untill they are collected.
7. Limbers for Lewis Guns will report at Coy H.Q. at
   13.30 hours for Lewis Guns. One Limber will be required
   for Canteen, 1 Limber for Orderly Room & Signalling Gear.
   Mess Cart, & Maltese Cart will report at respective places
   at 13.30. hours.
8. Riders for C.O. & M.O. will report at Bn H.Q. at 13.45 hours
   and Riders for Coy Comdrs. will report at Coy H.Q. at
   same hour.
9. One Officer & One N.C.O from each Coy will report to 2/Lt.
   H. Hannington. at Bn H.Q. as advance party to
   take over new Camp & Guide Coys & Bn H.Q. to billets.
   This party will report to 2/Lt. Hannington at 12.45. hours.
10. All Canvas, except that used by Q.M. Stores & Transport
    will be left standing.
11. Completion of Relief to be notified to Bn H.Q by
    Code word "DARBY."
12. Acknowledge.

                                        James Mann 2/Lt
                                        15 R. Innis. Fus.   Adjt.

Copy No.   1   C.O.
           2   O/c G. Coy
           3   O/c H "
           4   O/c I "
           5   O/c J "
           6   Transport Officer.
           7   Q. Master.
           8   R.S.M.
           9   War Diary.
          10   File
          11   Office.

"C" FORM.
MESSAGES AND SIGNALS.

Army Form C. 2121

Prefix SM	Code 1128	Words 40	Sent, or sent out.	Office Stamp.
Received from Juza	By W.R...		At ___ m.	Pomu
Service Instructions	Juza		To ___	17/10/18
			By	

Handed in at Juza Office 1128 m. Received 1200 m.

TO Pomu

Sender's Number	Day of Month	In reply to Number	AAA
G7/52	17		

Brigade will move tomorrow morning to Billets in Armentiers and Houplines aaa Billeting officers will meet Staff Capt at 1400 hours today at B23 D? 8 aaa Lieut Lewis Pomu will also be at Rendezvous aaa acknowledge

FROM Juza
PLACE & TIME

13th Bn Royal Inniskilling Fuslrs.
OPERATION ORDER No. 26

SECRET.   Copy No. 9

17.10.18.

Ref Map. Sheet 36 N.W. 1/20000.

1. The Bde will move tomorrow 18/10/18 to Billets in HOUPLINES and NOUVEL HOUPLINES.
2. The Battalion will move to Billets in Square C.21.d
3. The Battalion will be ready to move off at 0830 hours in the following order:—

    B.H.Qrs. H. I. J. & G Coys   Dress:- Fighting Order.

4. All tents, shelters etc will be struck and dumped at NISSON HUT beside H Coy by 0730 hours.
5. Only trench kits and small mess kits will be taken forward.
6. Officers' Valises, surplus kit, packs, and blankets (tied in bundles of 10) will be dumped at NISSON HUT beside H Coy at 0730 hours. A limber will call at Coy H.Qrs at 0715 hours for Officers' Valises etc.
   Sergt Roberts and 4 salvage men will mount guard at NISSON HUT over all stores dumped there. They will be rationed by Q.M. until further notice.
7. Each Coy will detail an Officer and 3. O.R. to proceed to HOUPLINES (square C.21d) at 0600 hours (tomorrow 18/10/18) to prepare billets for arrival of Battalion.
8. Transport will move via ERQUINGHEM, and will be brigaded under Lieut J.G. Lewis at C.27.a.0.5.
9. A limber will report tonight to H.Q. 119th T.M.B. Rations and forage for 3 days will be taken.
10. Rear Orderly Room will move to Transport Lines, and if possible Canteen.
11. Coys will report themselves in billets to Bn H.Q by Code Words "RATS".
12. Transport Officer will make all necessary arrangements re Transport.
13. Riders for C.O. M.O. & Coy Comdrs at 0815 hours. Mess Cart 0815 hours.
14. ACKNOWLEDGE.

Copy No. 1 o/c C.O. Coy
" 2 " G "
" 3 " H "
" 4 " I "
" 5 " J "
" 6 " Transport Officer
" 7 " Quartermaster
" 8 " R.S.M.
" 9 " War Diary
" 10 " File
" 11 " Office

James Mann
2/Lt
A/Adjt
13th Bn Royal Innis Fuslrs.

"C" FORM.
MESSAGES AND SIGNALS.

Prefix **SB** Code **0044** Words **78**

Received from **JUZA** By **JA Ellis**

Service Instructions **PRIORITY JUZA**

Sent, or sent out. At ___ m. To ___ By ___

Office Stamp. **Danu** **18/10/4**

Handed in at ___ Office ___ m. Received ___ m.

TO

Sender's Number.	Day of Month.	In reply to Number.	AAA
Cancel	0043	and	amendments
thereto	aaa Brigade	will move
to positions in	C 30 D	and
J 1 A	and D	today aaa
move to be	completed	by
1200	hours	aaa	Bde
Hqrs	will	open at	LA PREVOTE
in J 1 D	at 1100	Hours	aaa
transport	will	be Brigaded in
J 1 D	aaa	arrangments	for
dumping	Baggage	as	per
0043	stand	good	aaa
billetting	artists	will	meet
staff	captain	at	1000 Hours

FROM
PLACE & TIME

"C" FORM.
MESSAGES AND SIGNALS.

Army Form C. 2121
(In books of 150.)
No. of Message _____

Prefix _____ Code _____ Words _____	Sent, or sent out.	Office Stamp.
Received from _____ By _____	At _____ m.	Pony
Service Instructions	To _____	18/10/19
	By _____	

Handed in at _____ Office _____ m. Received _____ m.

TO

*Sender's Number.	Day of Month.	In reply to Number.	A A A
today	at	fork	roads
g 1 D 44	a a a	acknowledge	

FROM
PLACE & TIME   J 4 3 A

* This line, except AAA, should be erased if not required.

SECRET.
13th Bn. Royal Inniskilling Fusiliers
OPERATION ORDER.   No 27.
DATE Oct 23/1918.   COPY No 10.

Reference Map. Sheet 36. 1/40.000.

1. The Bde will march tomorrow Oct. 24. to the BONDUES Area. An advance Guard Scheme will be carried out in accordance with the move.

2. The Bde will march as under:—
   Advanced Guard.
                 13th E. Lancs. Regt.

   Main Body
       Bde. H.Q.   09.00. hours.
       T.M.B.   09.02. "
       13th R. Innis. Fus.   09.08. "
       12th N. Staffs. Regt.   09.18. "

   Starting Point. Road Junction J.1.d.u.u.
   Route. PERENCHIES — LA CROIX — FORT DUVERT. GALANT — WAMBRECHIES — E 27 c.o.u. — E 27 a 9.u. — E 21 — E 22 — BONDUES
   Distance between. Battns.   600 yds.
          "   "   Coys   100 "
          "   " Unit & Transport. 100 "

3. The Battn will fall in at 08.30. hours on the Road leading to J. Coy. in the following order
       Bn. H.Q.   I.   J.   G. & H. Coys.
   Dress:— FIGHTING ORDER.
   A halt will be made about midday for dinners.

4. Officers' Valises, mens' packs, & Blankets (tied in bundles of 10. with a label) will be stacked at Bn H.Q. by 07.30 hours (G. Coy will detail 1 n.c.o. and 1 man to remain with Kits until they are collected at 13.00 hours

5. 1st Line Transport will travel with Battn except baggage waggons which will travel in rear of main body.

6. Lt. J. S. Pirie will meet Staff Captain at Bavin...
Church at 10·00 hours tomorrow to arrange billeting.
7. Officers' Mess Kits will be dumped at Bn H.Q.
08.00 hours. No tables chairs etc to be taken forward.
8. Two Lorries will report at Bn. H.Q. at 13.00 hours
to take forward packs etc. to new camp. R.Q.M.S.
will remain and see that everything is taken
forward. One Lorry may do a second journey
if required.
9. Transport Officer will make all necessary
arrangements regarding transport. Mess Cart and
Maltese Cart at Bn. H.Q. at 07·45 hours.
10. Riders for C.O. & M.O.
  at 08.30. hours.
11. Certificates that Camp has been left thoroughly
clean will be handed to Adjutant on parade.
12. Acknowledge.

James Maw
2/Lt.
Act./Adjt.
13 Bn R. Innis Fus.

23/10/18.

Copy. No 1   C.O.
  "   " 2   O/C G. Coy.
  "   " 3   " H. "
  "   " 4   " I. "
  "   " 5   " J. "
  "   " 6   " Quarter Master
  "   " 7   " T. O.
  "   " 8   R.S.M.
  "   " 9   War Diary
  "   " 10   File.
  "   " 11   Office.

P.T.O

Addendum to Operation order No 29 d/23/10/18

Sub para 6. Add. One officer from each Coy will report to Lt. Petrie at 07.50 hours at Bn H.Q.

5 Riders to be at Bn H.Q. at 08.00 hours

"C" FORM.
MESSAGES AND SIGNALS.

Army Form C. 2123.
(In books of 100.)
No. of Message ....

Prefix **SM** Code **1035** Words **13**

Received from **JUZA** By **MILL BOY**

Service Instructions

Sent, or sent out.
At .... m.
To ....
By ....

Office Stamp.
25/10/18
POMU

Handed in at **JUZA** Office **1035** m. Received **1036** m.

TO **POMU**

Sender's Number.	Day of Month.	In reply to Number.	AAA
GT858	25		
Brigade	will	move	towards
on	26TH	to	WATTRELOS

FROM **JUZA**

PLACE & TIME

* This line, except AAA, should be erased, if not required.

"C" FORM.
MESSAGES AND SIGNALS.

Army Form C. 2123.

Prefix BM	Code 2037	Words 20	Sent, or sent out.	Office Stamp.
Received from JUZA	By Gleave		At ... m. To ... By ...	PONV 25/7/18

Service Instructions: JUZA

Handed in at ... Office ... m. Received 20·65 m.

TO: PONV

*Sender's Number.	Day of Month.	In reply to Number.	A A A
GT 871	26	—	

Ref 0045 today AAA POPA moves tomorrow to CROIX STA (L9 A H.Q.) instead of WATTRELOS area leaving main column at MOUVAUX

FROM: JUZA

PLACE & TIME:

"C" FORM.
MESSAGES AND SIGNALS.

Prefix SM	Code 185h	Words 31	Sent, or sent out.	Office Stamp.
Received from JU2A	By Bristow D		At ___ m.	POMU
Service Instructions JU2A			To ___	25/10/18
			By	

Handed in at ___ Office 1854 m. Received 1900 m.

TO   POMU

Sender's Number.	Day of Month.	In reply to Number.	A A A
ST867	25		
Ref	O O	45	aaa
Lorries	are	Detailed	as
under	aaa	Each	Battalion
one	aaa		available
To	Do two	journeys	aaa
Guides	will	Report	at
Bde	HQrs	06·00	hours

FROM   JU2A
PLACE & TIME

7 40
  10
  58
  ─
  40
  ──

  24
  ──

Secret

13th Bn Royal Irish Rifles
Operation Order No 28
October 25th 1918

Copy No. 11

Ref. Sheet 36)
       57) 40,000

1. The Bn will move tomorrow 26.10.18 to the
WATTRELOS area as under:—

                              Time past Str. Pr.
    Bn. H.Q.   09.00 hrs
    T.M.B.   09.0?
    13th R. Lancs Regt.   09.02 "
    12th W. Staffs Regt.   09.05 "
    13th R. Innis. Fus.   09.08 "
    TRANSPORT (in Brigade   09.11
              Ammunition
              cart columns)

    STARTING POINT X. Roads F.14.a.5.?
    ROUTE :— MOUVAUX — ROUBAIX.
    Distances between Bns   20 yards
                     Coys   10
    100 yards between every 12 vehicles of transport

2. The Bn will fall in on road leading to
Bn. H.Q at 07.15 hrs in the following order:—
    Bn. H.Q. T. C. W. X + I Coys.
    DRESS :—   Fighting Order.

3. Officers' valises, men's packs & blankets (tied
in bundles of 10) will be stacked at entrance
to HOSPICE by 0645 hrs (Each Coy will detail
1 N.C.O + 2 men to remain with kits until
they are collected).

4. 2/Lt H. Hannington and one officer from each
Coy will meet Staff Captain at the MAIRIE
(A.22.a.3.3) at 09.00 hours. These officers will
rendezvous at Bn. H.Q. at 07.00 hrs prompt.
bicycles at Bn H.Q.

5. Separate instructions have been issued
to Transport Officer.
R.Q.M.S. will remain until camp has been
cleared.

6. Riders for C.O, 2nd in Command, Adjt and 4 Coy Comdrs at 07.20 hours at Hospice.

7. Quartermaster will detail a guide to report to Bde H.Q at 09.00 hrs for lorry, to take Blankets & packs to new Camp. This lorry can do a second journey.

8. ACKNOWLEDGE.

James Mann
2 Lt
Act/Adjt
13th R. Innis Fus.

25/10/18.

Copy. No 1 - C.O
    2 - 2nd in Comd
    3 - O/c P. Coy
    4 - H
    5 - I
    6 - J
    7 - T.O
    8 - Q'Master
    9 - R.S.M
   10 - WAR DIARY
   11 - FILE

SECRET   13[?] [Infantry Brigade?]
                          Operation Order No. 29[?]

Ref map sheet 57 [?]/40000

1. The [Brigade?] will move [as under?]

                          Time past
                          Starting Point.   To: Route
   Bde H.Q.   10.00 hours.   LEERS NORD   A.29. a.v. LEERS.
   14th T.M.B.   10.04   "
   13th R. Innis. Fus.   10.07   "   NECHIN
   12th N. Staffs Regt.   10.14   "   NOUVEAU MONDE   NO RESTRICTIONS.
                                                 (B. 17 & 18 ards.)
   13th Bn. E. Lancs.   LEERS NORD   A.29. a.v. LEERS
        Starting Point — A.29. a.24.
        Distance between Battalions. 300 yards.
                          Coys.   10 yds.

2. The Batt. will assemble in the square WATTRELOS at [?]
   Formation - Close Column of Companies.   0945
   Dress - Fighting Order.

3. Officers valises, men's packs, blankets (tied in bundles of 10) will be
   stacked at Band stand by 0830 hours.

4. [?] Coy will detail 1 N.C.O. & men to guard his dump until
   everything has been collected.

5. First line transport will travel in rear of Batt.

6. Officers mess kits will be dumped at Bn. H.Q. [mess?] by 0830 hrs.
   Mess cart at Bn H.Q. mess at 0900 hours. Mules [cart?] [Red?] [Cross?]
   [?] at 0900 hours.

7. Separate instructions have been issued to Transport
   Officer.

8. Riders for C.O. Adjutant. M.O. 2d Coy. Comdr. [?] at 0930 hours

                          (Continued)

17

8. [?] personnel will report to O i/c at 0800 [...]

9. 2 Lorries O i/c report to the OC at 0800 to [...] to take packs, blankets etc to new area
   O.M. will detail a guide to report to Bde HQ. to [...] lorries to Band Stand.   These lorries will do a second journey if necessary.
   R.D. W.S. will remain until present area is cleared of all stores etc.

10. Acknowledge.

In the field
  Oct 31. 1918.

James Mann
Capt & Adjt
13 Bn R. [Irish?]

Copy No. 1 C.O.
        2 O.C. G Coy
        3 "   H Coy
        4 "   I "
        5 "   J "
        6 Transport Officer
        7 Q.M.
        8 R.S.M.
        9 War Diary
       10 Office
       11 File
       12

"C" FORM.
MESSAGES AND SIGNALS.

Army Form C. 2123.
(In books of 100.)
No. of Message..........

Prefix	Sol	Code	2010	Words		Sent, or sent out.	Office Stamp.
Received from		By	Bundell			At .... m.	
Service Instructions			TW2A			To	
						By	

Handed in at .... Office 810 m. Received 825 m.

TO .... Porte

Sender's Number.	Day of Month.	In reply to Number.	A A A
GT919	31		

Following lorries will report to Bde Hqrs at 1000 hrs tomorrow aaa guides should be sent to meet them aaa to do a journey aaa Lock bxr 2 aaa 1 x 2 timbers will report to NWE 0800 hrs tomorrow aaa One lorry will be at Bde Hq for NWE at about 800 hrs a guide should report at Bde Hq to meet it

FROM TW2A
PLACE & TIME

Confidential

War Diary
of
13th Bn. Royal Inniskilling Fusiliers

From 1/11/18 to 30/11/18.

(VOLUME 1).

Army Form C. 2118.

WAR DIARY
or
INTELLIGENCE SUMMARY.
(Erase heading not required.)

Instructions regarding War Diaries and Intelligence Summaries are contained in F. S. Regs., Part II. and the Staff Manual respectively. Title pages will be prepared in manuscript.

Place	Date	Hour	Summary of Events and Information	Remarks and references to Appendices
WATTRELOS	1/11/18	10.00	Battalion moved by march route to NECHIN	
NECHIN		11.30	Battalion arrived - Billets	
	2/11/18		110th Infantry Brigade Wiregram No. B.M.86 received.	
			" " " " B.M. 88 "	
	3/11/18		Carried on Battalion training.	
			110th Infantry Brigade OO.47 received (Copy attached)	
			OO.30 issued. (Copy attached)	
			Battalion won Silver Bugle for best singing Platoon in Brigade	
			2 Coys passed through Gas	
			2 Coys passed through "	
			Relieved 8th Royal West Surreys in Brigade Reserve	
	4/11/18		110th Infantry Brigade Wiregram B.M.94 received	
			" " " " B.M. 49	
			" " " " B.M. 45	
	5/11/18		Recef Order 8/4.5/G.L received	
			Instructions in case of advance issued.	

(A9479) Wt W4355/P360 600,000 12/7 D. D. & L. **Sch. 52a.** Forms/C2118/5.

Army Form C. 2118.

WAR DIARY
or
INTELLIGENCE SUMMARY.
(Erase heading not required.)

Instructions regarding War Diaries and Intelligence Summaries are contained in F. S. Regs., Part II. and the Staff Manual respectively. Title pages will be prepared in manuscript.

Place	Date	Hour	Summary of Events and Information	Remarks and references to Appendices
MECHIN	6/11/18		110th Infantry Brigade O.O. & B received.	
			Training carried on - 6 O.R. wounded	
	7/11/18		110th Infantry Brigade telegram B.M. 68 received	
			Carried on training	
	8/11/18		110th Infantry Brigade telegram S.A.A. 74 received.	
			" " " " B.M. 80	
			" " " " A/11	
			" " " " B.M. 82	
			" " " " G.T. 26	
	9/11/18		Battalion carried on march route	
			Nos. 4 Coy a & b Coys to PECQ. & Coys to WARCOING	
			Battalion crossed SCHELDT and moved to CHATEAU EN HAUT - J.4.a. ShU 37.	
Mart 37 J.4.a.			110th Infantry Brigade telegram B.T. 80 received.	
			" " " " B.M. 95	
			" " " " B.M. 97	
			" " " " B.M. 83	

Army Form C. 2118.

WAR DIARY
or
INTELLIGENCE SUMMARY.
(Erase heading not required.)

Instructions regarding War Diaries and Intelligence
Summaries are contained in F. S. Regs., Part II.
and the Staff Manual respectively. Title pages
will be prepared in manuscript.

Place	Date	Hour	Summary of Events and Information	Remarks and references to Appendices
	10/10/18		O.O. No. 30 issued	
			Battalion moved forward	
			110th Infantry Brigade Minimum B.M. 180 received	
			Battalion billeted at BOIS DE CHIN area.	
BOIS DE CHIN	11/10/18		110th Infantry Brigade M.O. No.11 received	
			"In Battalion area at 11 o'clock to-day"	
			Bivouac in forming	
	12/10/18		110th Infantry Brigade O.O. No. 4 received	
			O.O. No. 31 issued	
			Battalion moved by march route to MAROILLES	
	13/10/18		Carrier on Guard. 2 days upon rum fatale	
	14/10/18		110th Infantry Brigade M.O. Nos. 67, 31 & received. E.T. nos.	
			Carried on training	
	15/10/18		110th Infantry Brigade O.O. 50 received	
			Wigram O.68. received	

WAR DIARY
or
INTELLIGENCE SUMMARY.

(Erase heading not required.)

Army Form C. 2118.

Place	Date	Hour	Summary of Events and Information	Remarks and references to Appendices
BOIS de GHIN CROIX	15/11/18		C.O. 38 received.	
	16/11/18		Battalion moved by motor lorries to CROIX	
	17/11/18		Church Parade 10 a.m. Letter to abbé & Curé Church Parade.	
	18/11/18		Brigade Church Parade 11 a.m.	
	19/11/18		Caludé & training	
	20/11/18		" "	
	21/11/18		" "	Arden times Army school - Commissioned p
	22/11/18		" "	
	23/11/18		" "	
	24/11/18		" "	7 Officers of men to duty
	25/11/18		Received at Lezard Army Bay to the Mairie at ROUBAIX by B.O.C. Second Army - Guard	
	26/11/18		of Honor, of & drilldrum at 50 o.R. provided by Bo ball. Church Parade	
	27/11/18		Inspection of 119th Infantry Brigade by G.O.C. Actn Several Army relief	
	28/11/18		No Press Country Run Orders times Army school	
	29/11/18		Carried on Training	

Army Form C. 2118.

WAR DIARY
or
INTELLIGENCE SUMMARY.
(Erase heading not required.)

Instructions regarding War Diaries and Intelligence Summaries are contained in F. S. Regs., Part II. and the Staff Manual respectively. Title pages will be prepared in manuscript.

Place	Date	Hour	Summary of Events and Information	Remarks and references to Appendices
CROIX	28/4/18		Carried on training. Battalion Baths constructed.	Using Serries Army School
	29/4/18		Battalion does twenty firing. Attire between Army School	
	30/4/18		Carried on training. but Officers supervise the thing.	

Lieut. Col.
Comdg. 1/6 Battalion Royal Inniskilling Fusiliers

(A975) Wt W355/P360 600,000 12/17 D. D. & L. Sch. 52a. Forms/C2118/5.

Confidential

War Diary
of The
2.Bn. Royal Inniskilling Fusiliers

From 1/12/18 to 31/12/18.

(Volume 1)

WAR DIARY or INTELLIGENCE SUMMARY

Army Form C. 2118.

(Erase heading not required.)

Place	Date	Hour	Summary of Events and Information	Remarks and references to Appendices
CROIX	1/12/18		Carried on Battalion Training & Education.	TOPA
	2/12/18		Brigade Cross Country Race - Battn. won Silver Cup (1st team home) - 1 OR taken on Strength	TOPA
	3/12/18		Carried on Battalion Training & Education	TOPA
	4/12/18		Practice Ceremonial Parade at NECHIN - postponed owing to rain - 4 OR taken on Strength	TOPA
	5/12/18		Carried on Battalion Training & Education	TOPA
	6/12/18		Carried on Battalion Training & Education	TOPA
	7/12/18		Carried on Battalion Training & Education - 2 OR taken on Strength.	TOPA
	8/12/18		Brigade Ceremonial Parade - Medal Presentation. 2/Lt. SHARP MM + 2/Lt. SLADEN reported for duty	TOPA
			Lt.Col. J.F.PLUNKETT. DSO. MC. DCM. (Croix de Guerre - Gold Star)	TOPA
			48115 Sgt. Mennie MM. (Croix de Guerre)	TOPA
			48149 Corpl Gallacher. Military Medal	TOPA
			48012 Cullen " "	TOPA
			48244 L/Cpl Parrey " "	TOPA
			48240 Pte. Walsh " "	TOPA
			47422 Cpl. McLaren " "	TOPA
			47398 Pte. Scott " "	TOPA

WAR DIARY
or
INTELLIGENCE SUMMARY.

Army Form C. 2118.

Place	Date	Hour	Summary of Events and Information	Remarks and references to Appendices
CROIX	9/12/18		Carried on Battalion Training & Education.	T/180
			Brigade Football League won by the battalion.	T/180
	10/12/18		Carried on Battalion Training & Education – 4 OR taken on strength.	T/180
	11/12/18		Divisional Ceremonial Parade at NECHIN. – 30 OR to Demobilization Camp.	T/180
	12/12/18		Carried on Battalion Training & Education. – 3 OR to Demobilization Camp	T/180
	13/12/18		Divisional Cross Country Run. 1st 17th R.F.A. 2nd 13th R. Innis. Fus. – 30 OR to Demobilization Camp	T/180
	14/12/18		Carried on Battalion Training & Education – 13 OR to Demobilization Camp.	T/180
	15/12/18		Corps Ceremonial Parade at NECHIN – Postponed owing to rain.	T/180
			Divisional Church Parade ROUBAIX.	T/180
	16/12/18		Carried on Battalion Training & Education. 1 OR taken on strength – 9 OR to Demobilization Camp	T/180
	17/12/18		Corps Ceremonial Parade at NECHIN.	T/180
	18/12/18		Carried on Battalion Training & Education	T/180
			Divisional Cup Semi-Final. 17th R.F.A. v 6nls. 13th R. Innis. Fus. 1 goal.	T/180
	19/12/18		Carried on Battalion Training & Education. – 3 OR taken on strength.	T/180
	20/12/18		Carried on Battalion Training & Education – 4 OR taken on strength.	T/180
	21/12/18		Carried on Battalion Training & Education.	T/180

WAR DIARY or INTELLIGENCE SUMMARY

Army Form C. 2118.

(Erase heading not required.)

Place	Date	Hour	Summary of Events and Information	Remarks and references to Appendices
CROIX	22/12/18		Carried on Battalion Training & Education	T(K)
	23/12/18		Carried on Battalion Training & Education	T(K)
	24/12/18		Carried on Battalion Training & Education	T(K)
	25/12/18		Christmas day	T(K)
	26/12/18		Boxing Day	T(K)
	27/12/18		Carried on Battalion Training & Education	T(K)
	28/12/18		Carried on Battalion Training & Education -13 O.R. taken on Strength - 5 O.R. to Demobilization Camp	T(K)
	29/12/18		Carried on Battalion Training & Education	T(K)
	30/12/18		Carried on Battalion Training & Education - 1 O.R. to Demobilization Camp	T(K)
	31/12/18		Carried on Battalion Training & Education - 3 O.R. to Demobilization Camp	T(K)

T.C. Dickson ~ Major.
Comdg. 13th R. Cumbd. Fus.

Army Form C. 2118.

WAR DIARY
or
INTELLIGENCE SUMMARY.

(Erase heading not required.)

Place	Date	Hour	Summary of Events and Information	Remarks and references to Appendices
CROIX FRANCE	1/1/19		Carried on Training - 1 OR demobilizes	
	2/1/19		Carried on Training 2 OR demobilized	
	3/1/19		Carried on Training 2 OR taken on strength. 1 OR off strength - Hosp.	
	4/1/19		Carried on Training 1 OR taken on strength	
	5/1/19		Carried on Training 2 OR demobilizes	
	6/1/19		Carried on Training 1 OR demobilizes	
	7/1/19		Carried on Training 3 OR demobilizes	
	8/1/19		Carried on Training 3 OR demobilizes 4 OR off strength - Hosp.	
	9/1/19		Carried on Training 2 OR demobilizes	
	10/1/19		Carried on Training 4 OR taken on strength. 1 off strength - deceased. Leave. 2nd Lt. E. PEARSON taken on str.	
	11/1/19		Carried on Training 4 OR demobilizes. 3 off strength - Hosp.	
	12/1/19		Carried on Training Capt. (A/Major) T.C.N. DICKSON + 5. OR demobilizes	
	13/1/19		Carried on Training 2/Lt J.G.M. PARRY + 2 OR demobilizes	
	14/1/19		Carried on Training	
	15/1/19		Carried on Training 4 off strength - Hosp.	
	16/1/19		Carried on Training	

Army Form C. 2118.

WAR DIARY
or
INTELLIGENCE SUMMARY.
(Erase heading not required.)

Instructions regarding War Diaries and Intelligence Summaries are contained in F. S. Regs., Part II. and the Staff Manual respectively. Title pages will be prepared in manuscript.

Place	Date	Hour	Summary of Events and Information	Remarks and references to Appendices
CROIX FRANCE	17/1/19		Carried on Training	
	18/1/19		Carried on Training. 5 OR demobilized	
	19/1/19		Carried on Training. 8 OR demobilized. 1 OR taken on strength	
	20/1/19		Practice ceremonial parade ROUBAIX. 2/L A. BELL + 15 OR demobilized. 3 OR taken on strength	
	21/1/19		Presentation of King's Colours (Union Flag) by XV Corps Comdr on GRAND PLACE, ROUBAIX 2/L. T.D. STOCKS + 15 OR demobilized	
	22/1/19		Carried on Training. Lt. AY. SHILTON + 24 OR demobilized	
	23/1/19		Carried on Training. 9 OR demobilized	
	24/1/19		Carried on Training	
	25/1/19		Carried on Training 15 OR demobilized	
	26/1/19		Carried on Training 9 OR demobilized 3 OR taken on strength 2 OR taken on strength - Hosp	
	27/1/19		Carried on Training 2/Lt. HAWKINS + 28 OR demobilized	
	28/1/19		Carried on Training 26 OR demobilized 2/Lt KENNEDY demobilized	
	29/1/19		Carried on Training	
	30/1/19		Carried on Training	
	31/1/19		Carried on Training 1 OR on strength	

Confidential

War Diary
of the
13th Bn. Royal Innis. Fus.
1st to 28th Feb. 1919

(VOLUME II)

WAR DIARY

INTELLIGENCE SUMMARY

Army Form C. 2118.

(Erase heading not required.)

Instructions regarding War Diaries and Intelligence Summaries are contained in F. S. Regs., Part II. and the Staff Manual respectively. Title pages will be prepared in manuscript.

Place	Date	Hour	Summary of Events and Information	Remarks and references to Appendices
CROIX	1/2/19		Carried on training. 1 OR taken on strength. 12 OR demobilised	
	2/2/19		Carried on training. Lt. J.N. PETRIE M.C. + 8 OR demobilised	
	3/2/19		Carried on training. 13 OR demobilised	
	4/2/19		Carried on training.	
	5/2/19		Carried on training. 10 OR struck off strength	
	6/2/19		Carried on training. 2/Lt P.J. DALY + 21 OR demobilised	
	7/2/19		Carried on training. 10 OR demobilised	
	8/2/19		Carried on training. 7 OR demobilised	
	9/2/19		Carried on training. 1 OR taken on strength. 2/Lt J. FINNEY M.C. died. 11 CCS STANDAE. 6 OR demobilised	
	10/2/19		Carried on training. 19 OR demobilised	
	11/2/19		Carried on training.	
	12/2/19		Carried on training.	
	13/2/19		Carried on training. 3 OR struck off strength + hosp. 25 OR demobilised	
	14/2/19		Carried on training. 21 OR demobilised	
	15/2/19		Carried on training. 12 OR demobilised	
	16/2/19		Carried on training. 2 OR demobilised	

WAR DIARY
INTELLIGENCE SUMMARY

Army Form C. 2118.

Instructions regarding War Diaries and Intelligence Summaries are contained in F.S. Regs., Part II and the Staff Manual respectively. Title pages will be prepared in manuscript.

(Erase heading not required.)

Place	Date	Hour	Summary of Events and Information	Remarks and references to Appendices
Crois	17/2/19		Carried on training. 4 OR demobilized	
	18/2/19		Carried on training	
	19/2/19		Carried on training	
	20/2/19		Carried on training. 2 OR struck off strength. 1 OR demobilized	
	21/2/19		Carried on training. 3 OR demobilized	
	22/2/19		Carried on training. 1 OR demobilized	
	23/2/19		Carried on training	
	24/2/19		Carried on training. 1 OR taken on strength	
	25/2/19		Carried on training. 1 OR struck off strength. Deserter	
	26/2/19		Carried on training	
	27/2/19		Carried on training	
	28/2/19		Carried on training. 2 OR demobilized	

A.B. Rowan Major Comdg.
3rd Tyne Electrical Engineers

13th Div. R. ...

CONFIDENTIAL.

WAR DIARY

MARCH, 1919.

VOL. II

Army Form C. 2118.

WAR DIARY
or
INTELLIGENCE SUMMARY.
(Erase heading not required.)

Instructions regarding War Diaries and Intelligence Summaries are contained in F. S. Regs., Part II. and the Staff Manual respectively. Title pages will be prepared in manuscript.

Place	Date	Hour	Summary of Events and Information	Remarks and references to Appendices
CROIX	1/3/19		1. O.R. demobilized	
	2/3/19		6. O.R. demobilized	
	3/3/19		4. O.R. demobilized	
	4/3/19		2. O.R. demobilized	
	"		4. O.R. struck off strength	
	5/3/19		1 O.R. struck off strength. 2nd Lieut. P.A. Garrard struck off strength 5/3/19	
	6/3/19		2nd Lieut G.W. Clayton struck off strength	
	7/3/19		1 O.R. struck off strength	
	8/3/19		Inspection of Camp by Adjutant	
	9/3/19		Lieut. C.R. Watson, 2nd Lieut F.W. Sharpke and 10 O.R. demobilized	
	10/3/19		3. O.R. struck off strength	
	11/3/19		Major M. Matthews struck off strength 13/3/19	
	12/3/19		Carried on training	
	13/3/19		do	
	14/3/19		1. O.R. demobilized	
	15/3/19		Carried on training	

Army Form C. 2118.

WAR DIARY
or
INTELLIGENCE SUMMARY.
(Erase heading not required.)

Instructions regarding War Diaries and Intelligence Summaries are contained in F. S. Regs., Part II. and the Staff Manual respectively. Title pages will be prepared in manuscript.

Place	Date	Hour	Summary of Events and Information	Remarks and references to Appendices
CROIX	2/3/19		Carried on training.	
			Signed Lieut Colonel	
			Comdg. 13th Bn Royal Inniskilling Fusiliers	

Army Form C. 2118.

WAR DIARY
or
INTELLIGENCE SUMMARY.
(Erase heading not required)

Instructions regarding War Diaries and Intelligence Summaries are contained in F. S. Regs., Part II. and the Staff Manual respectively. Title pages will be prepared in manuscript.

Place	Date	Hour	Summary of Events and Information	Remarks and references to Appendices
CROIX	16/3/19		Church Parade	
	17/3/19		Parade of Cooks to Divisional Commander's Mount. 3 O.R. struck of strength	
	18/3/19		Carried on Training	
	19/3/19		do	
	20/3/19		do	
	21/3/19		do	
	22/3/19		Capt. C. Moger struck of strength as from 15/3/19. Lieut. E.F. McNamara struck of strength as from 24/11/18. 15. O.R. demobilized.	
	23/3/19		2nd Lieut. E.W. Boyle struck of strength as from 23/3/19. 1.O.R. struck of strength as from 6/3/19.	
	24/3/19		5 O.R. struck of strength	
	25/3/19		Carried on Training	
	26/3/19		Capt. T.J. Morris and Lieut. H. Harris and 56 O.R. struck of strength.	
	27/3/19		1 O.R. struck of strength	
	28/3/19		2nd Lieut. G. Sladen and 15 O.R. struck of strength	
	29/3/19		Carried on Training	
	30/3/19		Church Parade	

CONFIDENTIAL.

WAR   DIARY

of

the

13th Battn. THE ROYAL INNISKILLING FUSILIERS.

From 1st April 1919.

To   30th April 1919.

VOLUME   II.

Army Form C. 2118.

WAR DIARY
or
INTELLIGENCE SUMMARY.
(Erase heading not required.)

Instructions regarding War Diaries and Intelligence Summaries are contained in F. S. Regs., Part II. and the Staff Manual respectively. Title pages will be prepared in manuscript.

Place	Date	Hour	Summary of Events and Information	Remarks and references to Appendices
CROIX FRANCE (NORD)	1/4/19		Training	
	2/4/19		Training & Recreation	
	3/4/19		Training	
	4/4/19		Training. 2/Lt. H. SHARP MM Demobilized	
	5/4/19		Training & Recreation. 9 O.R. transferred to 1/8 R. Innis. Fus	
	6/4/19		Divine Service	
	7/4/19		Training & Recreation	
	8/4/19		Training	
	9/4/19		Training & Recreation. 5 O.R. demobilized	
	10/4/19		Training	
	11/4/19		Training	
	12/4/19		Training & Recreation. 1 O.R. to H.Q. N°2 Cadre Group 40th Division	
	13/4/19		Divine Service	
	14/4/19		Training & Recreation. 1 O.R. taken on strength. Major L.C.ISADH MC & Lt H.E.McMAHON Cross-posted to 8th R. Irish Regt	
	15/4/19		Training. 2 O.R. demobilized	
	16/4/19		Training & Recreation	

WAR DIARY
INTELLIGENCE SUMMARY.
(Erase heading not required.)

Army Form C. 2118.

Place	Date	Hour	Summary of Events and Information	Remarks and references to Appendices
CROIX FRANCE (NORD)	17/4/19		Training. 2 O.R. taken on Strength.	
	18/4/19		Training. 2 O.R. to 1/5th R. Innis Fus.	
	19/4/19		Training & Recreation. 1 O.R. demobilised.	
	20/4/19		Divine Service	
	21/4/19		Training & Recreation	
	22/4/19		Training. 2/Lieut (A/Capt.) S. Smiles M.C. & 2/Lieut (A/Capt.) J.G. Lewis transferred to P.O.W. Coys	
	23/4/19		Training & Recreation. 2 O.R. taken on Strength	
	24/4/19		Training. 1 O.R. demobilised whilst on leave to U.K. 2 O.R. to 1/5th R. Innis Fus.	
	25/4/19		Training	
	26/4/19		Training & Recreation	
	27/4/19		Divine Service	
	28/4/19		Training	
	29/4/19		Training	
	30/4/19		Training & Recreation	

James Irvine Capt.
Comdg. 13th R. Innis Fus.

www.ingramcontent.com/pod-product-compliance
Lightning Source LLC
Chambersburg PA
CBHW081546160426
43191CB00011B/1855